THE SPIRIT SPEAKS

The Silver Birch Books

Teachings of Silver Birch   first published in 1938
Guidance from Silver Birch   first published in 1966
Philosophy of Silver Birch   first published in 1969
More Philosophy of Silver Birch   first published in 1979
Light from Silver Birch   first published in 1983
Silver Birch Companion   first published in 1986
A Voice in the Wilderness   first published in 1986
The Seed of Truth   first published in 1987
The Spirit Speaks   first published in 1988
Lift up your Hearts   first published in 1990

The cassette, "Silver Birch Speaks", recorded at the Hannen Swaffer Home Circle, is available from the publishers Psychic Press Limited.

THE SPIRIT SPEAKS

Compiled by
TONY ORTZEN

Psychic Press Ltd,
2 Tavistock Chambers,
Bloomsbury Way,
London WC1A 2SE

First published in 1988
This impression 1995

© Psychic Press Ltd

All rights reserved. No portion of this book may be reproduced or utilised in any form or by any means, electronic or mechanical, including photocopying, recording or retrieval system, without the prior permission in writing of the publisher. Nor is it to be otherwise circulated in any form or binding or cover other than that in which it is published.

ISBN 0 85384 073 3

Printed by Booksprint, West Street, St Philips, Bristol

THE SPIRIT SPEAKS

The publication of this book has been made possible
by the generous support of the following patrons:

London Spiritual Mission
P. J. Grimes
Mrs J. Whitehead
P. Russell
Hailsham Spiritualist Church
Lynn and Evelyn Hertsgaard
Mrs M. Merritt
Edmonton SNU Church
Spiritual Truth Foundation
Janet Mercer

CONTENTS

Introduction		1
1	'Souls are being touched'	5
2	'When knowledge reigns'	29
3	'The light and the shade'	38
4	'Love is the key'	54
5	'There is no judgement'	68
6	'Knowledge dispels fear'	82
7	'To master eternal truths'	104
8	'The riddle of life'	124

INTRODUCTION

THIS morning I took my dog for a walk. "Well," you might say with a certain justification, "what is so special about that?" But perhaps I should explain that my walk took me along the beach opposite to where I live. It was early. A slight haze hung far off over the horizon, yet to be dislodged by the rising sun. Human companions were few, just a handful of other devoted dog owners similarly taking their charges for a stroll. Nonetheless, there was company aplenty in the shape of seagulls, swooping, diving, circling and literally stretching their wings, as their plaintive cries mingled with the sound of the chill wind.

As I walked along the shore the ever-changing sea, in lazy mood, could hardly be bothered to move. It all seemed a gigantic effort. Yet the subdued waves ebbed and flowed, back and forth, grey and white, each time dragging a few reluctant rust and cream coloured pebbles with them.

Later still I sat in the square and watched a butterfly almost dancing in the sun. All around were signs of the season: the daffodils lifting their joyous yellow faces to the sun; the burgeoning honeysuckle swaying its green leaves in the wind; the tulips forcing their way through the earth; the birds serenading each other; the cottonwool-like clouds making their slow way across the by now azure sky.

Now it is rapidly approaching dusk, the day is almost done.

My cats are basking in the sun's dying rays, the dog sits contentedly, well walked, well fed. But my morning stroll and sojourn in the garden square contains a lesson for us all.

For no matter what may transpire, the sea will ebb and flow; the sun will rise, freely give its warmth, and silently set to be replaced by a glowing moon; the butterflies and birds will appear; the daffodils, tulips, honeysuckle and countless other plants, shrubs and trees will beckon to nature's call and bloom. Dogs and cats—like humans—will be born, enjoy the seasons of life and pass on to a world beyond, so near, so far.

In a nutshell what I am trying to convey is that all life is governed by natural law, a point made so eloquently, forcibly and repeatedly by Silver Birch. Truly can nothing—or no one—be above The Law.

This is the fifth Silver Birch book I have compiled, and for which I can take no credit. In short it is an amalgamation of two much earlier volumes, Sylvia Barbanell's "Silver Birch Speaks Again" and William Naylor's "Anthology of Silver Birch." To these I have deliberately added further material from the archives at "Psychic News," featuring as they do many questions put to the ever-patient spirit sage.

I have chosen the title "The Spirit Speaks" for that is exactly what Silver Birch did. Though his immediate mission ended in 1981 when Maurice Barbanell, his medium, passed, the guide's words are now probably read by more people in more countries than ever before. For neither Silver Birch's timeless teachings nor his profound, simply expressed philosophy know no earthly cultural, religious or man-made barriers.

As an entrée to this volume, let me quote what Silver Birch said of spirit power:

"The power of the spirit is here to stay in your world. It has made its mark; it will not depart. Throughout all ages attempts were made to secure a permanent lodgement of spirit power so that all the earthly children could have access to the Great Spirit and to His infinity of wisdom and knowledge and love.

"So many obstacles and barriers and handicaps have been overcome. All over the world of matter there are secure entrenchments that will never be dislodged again. No matter what popes, priests, statesmen or politicians may say the power of the spirit will not vanish from the world of matter.

"Spirit power is constant and abiding. It may ebb and flow, as its volume decreases and increases according to the conditions, but the power is always there engulfing you in its embrace of the love of those who have appointed themselves your guardian angels."

Tony Ortzen

Chapter 1

'SOULS ARE BEING TOUCHED'

NOTHING gave Silver Birch greater pleasure than speaking to mediums and spirit healers, who respectively prove survival to the grieving and are often able to effect cures and betterment even when medical science has tried—and failed.

So it was that world famous healer Harry Edwards—with his then assistants George and Olive Burton—were assured of a warm welcome when they paid a visit to Hannen Swaffer's home circle. And though he, too, is now in the spirit world he served faithfully for decades, Harry Edwards' healing ministry is being continued at Shere, Surrey, by his chosen successors Ray and Joan Branch.

"Great as is the work that has been achieved, the crown is still to be attained," said Silver Birch in greeting his visitors.

"You are coming into the fullness of your labours," added the guide. "All that has gone before is the preparation. Just as John the Baptist paved the way for the coming of the Nazarene, so the past years have paved the way for the coming events, for greater power to descend and work with you.

"The willingness, the sacrifice, the trust which has attained almost to perfection, these bring their own reward. Coalescence of the power of the spirit and the earthly forces becomes closer and closer, with the result that very often you have what seems the impossible taking place. I would like you to observe the great speed in which this can be attained when the conditions are right."

"We have seen that," said Edwards.

"So rejoice that great progress is being made," Silver Birch continued, "that souls are being touched and the incentive is being provided to others to strive to attain this measure of success. Keep your eyes on the one purpose, and that is to awaken souls to the reality of life. That is the reason, the main reason, for all spirit activity. Nothing else matters. The healing, the comfort that is attained through mediumship, the varying kinds of phenomena, all these draw attention to the message, that all who live are part of the Great Spirit, spiritual beings, and they must realise that so that they shall claim their heritage and fulfil their destiny.

"I know it is not easy always to do this work, but sometimes the greater the task the greater the difficulties that stand in the way. Spiritual attainment is not easy. It is a lonely path; it must be so. If all the great heights to which humanity can ascend were easy of attainment, they would not be worthwhile. The soul finds itself, not through ease, not through leisure, not through idleness, but through toil and striving and difficulty. It was never intended to be easy.

"Those who see you perform your acts of healing, and think how easy this all is, are only looking at the surface. They forget that behind it all there are the years of struggle before the present pinnacle has been reached. While they may be satisfied, you must not be. You must realise that every peak when it is reached reveals another peak that has to be scaled as well. I hope that helps you. I expect you know all this already."

"Yes, but it is good to know it again," said Edwards.

"The great value of our meeting like this is that we, who are not in your world, can remind you of the eternal principles, the unfailing spiritual truths, the foundation upon which we all rest. You who are encased in matter and have to face the daily problems and obstacles of your material bodies sometimes become so engrossed with these purely material things that you lose sight of the great spiritual realities behind them.

"How easy it is to think of the body as the individual, and this world in which you live as the reality, and not to realise the truth, which is that your world is the shadow and that your body is but the instrument of a much larger self. If only every hour of the day each one of you had the true perspective and could view every problem that arose in the light of spiritual knowledge, how much easier it would be; but, alas, it is not so.

"Even those who are engaged in the great task of co-operating with the power of the spirit forget, again and again, their primary obligations and are unable to measure up to the standard that their knowledge requires of them. Knowledge is a great teacher, a great helper, but it is always a great responsibility as to what you will do with the knowledge that you have attained.

"I know that in the course of your labours you will meet with many problems, some that will seem almost impossible to explain, some that will puzzle you, but this must be so. We are confronted again and again with the human element in your world and in ours. The law is perfect, but it has to work through imperfect beings, and it is impossible to predict with mathematical certainty what will happen with the law when it has to operate through human beings.

"Circumstances arise that thwart even the best laid plans. Sometimes I have seen it happen after many long years of preparation that the one who is chosen for the task decides according to his free will not to go ahead and all that is wasted. But we can rejoice at the measure of spirit power that is at work and we can rejoice that it is increasing in intensity. The fact that you can relieve and cure, the fact that you can help the suffering, the fact that this work grows and does not lessen, the fact that many come to you seeking, even though they may do so as their very last resort, all these are indications that the power of the spirit is spreading.

"I am one of those who contends that, once an individual has been touched by the power of the spirit, he can never be the same again. It brings to bear an influence that cannot be described, or even forgotten."

"On that last point it seems to me we want to have healing and preaching combined," the healer commented. "There seems to be no spiritual upliftment as far as the person is concerned."

"Not visibly," was the reply, "but there is an unseen influence at work all the time. The power of the spirit is magnetic and you cannot break that magnetic link once it has been made. The mere fact that an individual has been through your hands—I use the word 'hands' in the symbolic sense because they need not actually be personally treated— means that he has made his own link, that the spirit magnet has joined the metal and it will never be separated.

"To those who can see with the eyes of the spirit, with clairvoyance, the dark patch shows a little light. It is the first glimmer of understanding. It is as if the seed has pushed its head above the ground. It has emerged out of the darkness for the first time.

"That is what you achieve. It is very good to have the body put right, no one will dispute that, but it is much more important that the soul shall come into its own, and by bringing it in touch with itself, to use the words of the Bible, finding itself. You have placed it for the first time on the road that leads to understanding."

Here a member of the circle commented, "Very often some people think that a process of magic has been achieved. They think of the healer as a magician, not an instrument of the Great Spirit."

"I do not counsel it," replied the guide, "because if you try to combine the two it might be to the detriment of what is more important for them at that moment. If you lay stress on the fact that you are instruments of the power of the spirit, it may not sink in all at once, but you have started them thinking."

"What we find supporting the evidence of the continuance of spirit power is that, at times, people who ask for help write a year later to say they have got better," Edwards told the guide.

"That always must be," declared Silver Birch, "because what you cannot control is the measure of the spiritual unfoldment of the individual. I have touched on this before, but all is controlled by the evolution of the soul. That is the decisive factor. No soul can obtain for itself that to which it is not entitled. The body is but the servant of the spirit; it is not the master."

"Do you mean that an unevolved soul cannot be helped by spirit healing?" asked the healer.

"Yes, that is precisely what I mean," said Silver Birch, "but 'unevolved' is a difficult word. You must appreciate that when I speak of the law I do not refer to one law. I refer to the law which comprises all the natural laws of the universe. These conform to a perfect pattern. They are laws within laws all the time. The universe is boundless; no one can see its limit. The universe, like the Great Spirit, is infinite; the laws of the Great Spirit are infinite too and progress is an infinite process.

"Every person in the world of matter is a soul in a body. Now that soul is at a certain stage of evolution. You cannot dismiss the past life; it must come into the picture. The body is an expression of the mind, which in its turn is the expression of the spirit. The body represents the stage that the spirit has attained. If that soul is not to be healed because the pain is an essential concomitant of the process of purification that the soul must pass through in order to be ready for its next stage, then the power that flows through you cannot touch it, and there is no healer who can touch it.

"Pain is part of nature's process; pain is part of the law; pain, sorrow, suffering, these are all part of the natural law. You are back to what I have always tried to tell you that sunshine and shadow, peace and storm, light and darkness, love and hatred, all these are parts of the law; you cannot have one without the other."

"Pain is the result of breaking the law," commented a member of the circle.

"Do not use the words 'breaking the law'—say transgressing it," averred the guide. "But then you can only learn about the law through transgression sometimes. You are not perfect beings, you have the seed of perfection which is growing, but it can only grow through the variety of conditions that life imposes. If there were no pain, no storm, no difficulty, no suffering, no disease, the soul could not grow.

"The law cannot fail. If the law could fail then the Great Spirit would cease to be the Great Spirit and the universe would cease to have any harmony, rhythm of purpose. You must pin your whole faith on the exactness and perfection of the natural law, because there are stages where you cannot have knowledge and you must rely on faith. I never decry faith born of knowledge. I decry blind faith which becomes mere credulity. But you cannot have all the knowledge and so you must perforce rely on some faith to help you. I do not want, as a result, that you should avoid compassion or mercy or tenderness and say, 'This is the result of the law, I can do no more.' That would be wrong. You must strive to do your utmost, because in your striving you are fulfilling your own spiritual obligations."

After answering some questions Silver Birch stated: "The soul makes its own path. In addition to that, the body of matter imposes some restriction and limitation on the soul. The machine owes its existence to the spirit. There is a double influence at work the whole time, but overriding all is the influence of the soul. The soul is pre-eminent. This must be so because the soul is the Great Spirit within you and everything the Great Spirit possesses you possess in miniature."

"It seems very fundamental," Edwards declared. "You said that upon the state of the evolution of the soul depends whether healing can take place. If that is so, then we should devote more time to the healing of the mind rather than physical healing."

The guide asked, "Where do you think your healing power is exerted now if not on the spirit of those who come to you?"

"Through healing, the spirit self is healed and from that the physical healing takes place," replied Edwards.

"Yes, that is what I say," the guide pointed out.

"Is it not necessary for us to influence the physical mind?" Edwards inquired.

The guide answered: "The physical mind is but the servant of the spirit. If you get the spirit mind to work all the rest will follow, but if the spirit has not attained the stage of evolution where it can respond then you cannot make it work. The soul must advance still further. It will have to endure those processes which will shape it, and these are the painful ones. The soul cannot awaken in conditions of ease."

A member of the circle asked, "Do you mean that if the soul has not reached the necessary stage of evolution, even the influence of the healers from the spirit side cannot help?"

"It is the same law which applies to you and to us," answered Silver Birch.

"Isn't this what Christian Scientists believe?" another person asked.

"All truth is truth," the guide answered. "Labels do not matter, it is the principle with which we are concerned. If the one who is called a Christian Scientist can get the power of the spirit to work and, as a result of the life-giving, dynamic, vital forces, make the body obey and the cure is achieved, it matters not whether you call it spirit healing or Christian Science, does it?"

"I know that we play a part," said Edwards, "but it is very difficult for us to reach the soul of the patients."

"You do play a part, a very important part. If you were not there it could not happen. You are the instruments; you are the mediums; you are the condensers; you are the means by which the power is transmitted."

"Transmitted to what, the body or the soul?" asked the healer.

"I am not concerned with bodies," said the guide. "What makes an arm locked?"

"The physical state of the arm," Edwards replied.

"What has happened to that normal, healthy force which gives movement to the arm?"

"It has gone; it has surrendered to the disease; it has created the ill-condition."

"If that vitality could circulate, once again, what would happen?"

"The arm would get better."

"How do you get the life force to circulate through the arm?"

"That is their problem, not mine."

"You cannot do it by pushing the arm."

"Not by force."

"Not by force. But if the soul, which made the body in the first instance to be its instrument, can now pursue its old function and allow the force to function, where there is now a lock, health will result."

"That is what we see."

Another visitor to the circle asked, "Is the function of the healer to give stimulus to the natural resources of the patient?" Silver Birch answered:

"It is a little more than that, because the power of the spirit has to be stepped down owing to the fact that the patient is a spirit in a body in an earthly world, vibrating at a rate much lower than the power which has to reach him. The healers, who are the transformers, enable the power to be stepped down, and when the soul is ready healing is almost instantaneous; because of the degree of harmony between you and those that work with you the power can flow with lightning rapidity. If the soul of the patient cannot receive that force, there is nothing you can do. You cannot transfer the dynamic into the bent leg; it is only the soul of the patient that can do that."

Still the comments came, one visitor declaring, "Some people who say they do not believe in God are healed."

"Yes, because whether they believe in the Great Spirit or not, the law can operate," the guide said.

"But you would not think their souls would be evolved enough."

"You can have a great soul, who is an agnostic, and you can have a poor soul, who is religious. The greatness of the soul is not measured by belief, but by action. Listen, you can only help those who are ready to be helped. Rejoice at the fact that so many can be helped to find the light. It should be a measure of great satisfaction that through your instrumentality there are so many souls who are freed and who can rejoice because their feet have been placed on the pathways that lead to knowledge, to understanding and to abiding peace. That is the measure of the success. You will not be able to help them all; it is part of the law. I do not say that you should be satisfied—just as I say that the Great Spirit is in love and hatred, in sunshine and in storm. Success and failure again play their part, for if there were no failures there could be no successes."

Next came these questions: "Why is it that some people who believe and have faith and knowledge do not respond as well as they ought to spiritual healing? Is it a question of their soul?"

"Yes, it always comes back to the same thing. It is not a question of belief, faith, love. It is a question of that soul and what the soul is entitled to receive as a result of the stage it has reached in its evolution."

"We can see physical laws, but we cannot see the change to spirit laws," said Edwards.

"Even if you had many clairvoyants around you, they would not all see the same process at work. It is a most complex process. Do not think for a minute that it is simple. The whole of the interaction between matter and spirit is profound and complex. The body itself is a complicated piece of machinery and the spirit, too, is full of many facets. All of these are subject to laws that work within laws. Whilst harmony rules throughout, within the framework of all these laws there is plenty of interplay and the one reacts upon the other."

Olive Burton asked, "Did you say that the physical suffering of a person does not affect the spirit?"

"No, I did not say that. Any suffering to the body affects the spirit and suffering to the spirit affects the body. You cannot divorce one from the other. You are one person. Your body is part of you because it is a means by which you express yourself. You are the spirit. What happens to your body affects the spirit."

Next she asked, "If we make intercession for spirit help for people dying in agony, and the help cannot be given to keep them in this life, do you sometimes dissociate the spirit from the body to prevent any detrimental effect on the spirit?"

"That depends on the individual. The soul will be released from the body when the natural law determines it, unless you jump ahead of the natural law and force a severance, as does happen many times."

"We have had instances where we have thought that happened."

"Remember that in all such cases there is a law of balance at work; there is a shock to the spirit, though not a great one."

"Is it a shock caused by the early releasing?"

"That is so. In all things there are compensation and retribution. If the soul frees itself from the body before its proper time, it has an adjustment to make. It must depend on the individual circumstance. Where you can help is that, if the soul has earned the right, you can ease the pain, the adjustment is made and it is cushioned off, as it were, until it finds its proper status."

"If there is a condition where the patient is in such a state that there is no hope, is it a good or bad thing to hasten the end?" asked Edwards.

"I am one of those who always believe that the body should fall away when the spirit is ready to permit it."

"You hasten the break if you hasten the end of the physical body," said the healer. "Is that a right thing to do if there is great pain and suffering and there is not much chance of living?"

"I know the difficulty and I do not wish to appear to be stony-hearted in this matter. The law is quite clear and the body should fall away when the spirit is ready, just as the apple drops from the tree when it is ripe. If the apple drops before it is ripe it is not good for the apple. I am pointing out what should take place within the framework of natural law.

"There is the circumstance where through drugs and poisons the body becomes full of disease. The body was not intended to be riddled with disease; the laws have been transgressed, and so we go from stage to stage. Doesn't this point out what the natural result should be, no interference by the individual, by the doctor, or by anybody? All must come within the framework of natural law.

"It must produce an effect. As to whether it is good or bad, these can be determined by the knowledge of spiritual realities. It is not what is good for the body but what is best for the spirit, for what is best for the spirit must be best for the body."

On another occasion when Edwards and the Burtons were present the guide emphasised: "The true aim of the power of the spirit is to touch the souls of those who come within your ministry. Until the people of your world realise that they are souls and not physical bodies, they are going through life completely indifferent to reality; they are living in the shadows and chasing illusions. It is only when they become aware of their real selves, their spiritual natures, that they come face to face with reality. To find yourself is the object of all earthly life, because once you find yourself you will then, if you are wise, proceed to develop that divinity which lies within you. It is mostly true that in your world people do not find themselves, and are unaware of their spiritual nature until some sorrow or tragedy touches them. It is only in the darkness of life that light is found.

"You meet mostly those who are afflicted in body and mind and the healing should induce in them a realisation that they are spiritual beings, and if you can touch their spiritual natures, if you can kindle the divine spark, the flame will come in time and its illumination will brighten the whole of their lives. Now that is not always easy. You may succeed in putting right a limb that is misplaced, or clearing up a disorderly condition, but if in so doing the individual is aware that he is a spirit with a body, not a body with a spirit, then you are indeed performing the greatest service that is possible.

"You must appreciate that we are more concerned with the spirit than with the body. If the spirit is right, then the body will be right, but if the spirit is not right, not in true alignment, then the body cannot possibly be right. I would like you to appreciate this because it is an aspect of your labours that you cannot measure. The gratitude and thankfulness of those who obtain a cure, or relief, or a betterment, is as naught compared with the soul being touched and the releasing of that tremendous dynamic that is within them.

"It is not an easy task on which you are engaged; it demands great sacrifice and service. It is performed amidst difficulty and the pathway is not an easy one. But the path of the pioneer is never easy, neither is the road of those who give service one that is freed from obstacles. You must not expect that it should be so. Each obstacle and difficulty is a challenge to your own nature that you should rise triumphant above it and allow the pure gold of the spirit to be exhibited."

Here Harry Edwards asked, "With the healing of the mind, or the healing of the soul, is that not done more from your side than from ours?"

"Yes, it must be so," the guide replied.

"Is the part we play very little?"

"It is little and large," answered Silver Birch. "It is all a question of attunement. If you realise what takes place, it is a question of stepping down or lowering the vibration, frequency or radiation of these healing forces which, as you know, are differing kinds of rays, to a potential that can be manifested in physical form. That is one way. The other method is by using rays which produce a direct effect either on the mind or the spirit, that is, the consciousness of the sufferer, thus allowing the natural curative power to get rid of any disharmony or disease. That does not sound very clear."

"Yes it is clear, but its application is not so easily seen," Edwards commented.

"Let me put it another way," said the guide. "Nobody in your world knows what life is. It cannot be resolved into a physical, chemical or scientific explanation. Life eludes because life cannot be resolved into any material formula. Now we say that life is spirit and spirit is life. That power of the spirit which is released in your activity is life itself—the same power that enables individuals to have consciousness, to breathe, to move, to walk, to think, to reflect, the same power that enables the whole of the natural phenomena of life to perform and fulfil their functions, the same power that enables the tree to grow, the rose to bloom, the tide to ebb and flow. It is all part and parcel of the same power of the spirit.

"What makes you live is the fact that you are a spirit. It is in essence that that power, in varying degrees, according to the development, the evolution of the patient, is released.

Healing consists in applying this power to the soul of the patient where it is a disease that has its origin in the soul and not the body. As you know, there are two kinds of diseases, those that begin in the mind or the spirit, and those that are purely physical. The physical ones require the healer's touch, and those that owe their origin to mental or spiritual processes require the application of the power of the spirit.

"There is a limitation imposed by a set of factors; your own evolution, the evolution of your two collaborators, and the evolution reached by the person who comes for healing. What I call the karmic law is also at work, a process of cause and effect all the time."

"There are many diseases of the mind or the soul, but they have different effects on the body," said the healer. "I assume, therefore, that there must be qualitative healing forces to deal with the individual healing condition."

"Yes, that is perfectly true," said the guide. "Man is a triune being. Primarily, man is a spirit, that is the seed, the foundation of existence. Spirit is the first cause. This spirit is expressed through mind, which is the centre of consciousness, and mind regulates the body, which is the physical apparatus. Mind, spirit and body are interrelating factors that affect one another. Not only does mind affect the body, the body qualifies the mind; you cannot have one without the other."

"That works both ways," said Edwards.

"Yes," agreed Silver Birch, "the limitation of the mental and spiritual expression of the individual affect the body, and the body can be regulated to a height as yet unknown by the mind and the spirit. Study the fakirs who train themselves to have a complete mastery and discipline over their bodies. They can perform bodily feats that to the eyes of the Western world are impossible. That merely means that they have trained the mind to rule the body with a consciousness, a deliberate consciousness, that is not usually done."

Edwards asked, "If you kindle that consciousness within the spirit, as we may do, is not the spirit a dominant factor in the individual and could it not be more easily done from your side than from ours?"

Silver Birch answered: "In some cases Yes, but in the majority of cases No, because, like the many individuals who come to our world, although they are no longer on earth they are still nearer to earth than they are to spirit. Their evolution is so comparatively low that they are unable to respond to spiritual stimuli. Where you have this condition in your world we cannot reach them. That is what your mediumship consists of; it is the nexus, the stepping down process. The attuned medium, the evolved medium, is able both to reach out to spirit and to respond to matter.

"That is why it is very important that the healer, or the medium of any kind who desires to achieve the greatest results, should also strive to develop his own spiritual nature. It must be so that the higher you reach spiritually, the greater is the good that you can do because your range is extended. It is part of the law. As a corollary, it must be emphasised, too, that this process of development is a lonely path in which, as the individual unfolds, he leaves familiar signposts behind. I think you appreciate that; you cannot have one without the other."

Edwards intervened with: "You said of the healing rays, in one aspect of them, that they come and affect the physical body. Can you give me an indication where or how the change takes place between a spirit healing force and the physical change? There must at some time come the linking-up, where the spirit can be converted into matter? Can you give me any indication where the link is."

The guide answered: "It depends on the kind of healing that is to be performed. Some will find it hard to believe this, but in some cases the centres are the old ones laid down by the masters of wisdom. The 'third eye' and the solar plexus are used because these are centres where body, mind and spirit link up. As an alternative, the subconscious mind of the individual, where it is receptive, is acted upon in such a way so that it is stimulated into sending the necessary chemical reaction to the affected part in a manner that it would normally do if health were there and not disease."

Edwards said: "It is clear, but I still cannot see where the 'no man's land' is. Can you give me an indication of a more tangible link between the physical condition and the spirit healing force? There must be somewhere, some manner, where they change."

The guide replied: "That is rather difficult, my son, because it is not possible to explain it in a manner that I think I could make you understand it, but it is somewhat akin to what I think in your world is called a condenser, the function of a condenser being to regulate the transmission of one frequency into another. That is what mediumship is. In some cases, what you call ectoplasm is used, but not in the form in which it is used at a seance to reproduce a voice, or for materialisation, but in a more invisible——"

"An in-between state?" suggested Edwards.

The answer was, "Yes, where it is sufficiently plastic and malleable to spirit influence but yet sufficiently semi-physical to work in the material world. It is your power combined with it that acts as the condenser. Then this healing force actually flows into the individuals either through the pineal gland or the solar plexus. The vital force streams through their whole being and that is when they feel this warm electrical vibration.

"What you have to appreciate is that there is no set method. It is all a question of experiment. Every time you have healing you attract more and more what you would call scientists from our world. They have noted the reactions; what rays have been used; they have measured them; and that is why you have found a quickening in the results. You have noticed, for example, that often there is a healing before the patient comes on to the platform, and that will continue. The greatest part of your work is done, not in public, but in the silence of your soul."

Edwards said: "That does lead me to another question. There is an idea prevalent—you have just spoken of the gathering of scientists on your side—that there is conflict between various healing guides should one of our patients receive absent healing from us and physical healing from another medium. It seems to me to be contrary to all spiritual law. What do you think?"

The guide answered, "I say let the results determine it."

"But that is not an argument that we can use."

"In some cases there is a conflict and in other cases there is no conflict. This cannot be laid down because there is a varied set of circumstances with every patient. You cannot look at an individual and say if he comes to you you will heal him. It may be that the stage of evolution he has reached and you have reached will determine that you can succeed, and it may be that you can partially help and others, with another set of conditions, can go a stage further. The more one sees of the working of this simple but intricate process, the more one guards oneself against laying down arbitrary laws. The power of the spirit is infinite in its variety of manifestations. The wisest plan is not to assert what must and what must not be. There are certain essentials of motive and desire to serve, but after that who is to say what will succeed or what will not succeed?"

Edwards said: "We are not concerned with the details, but with the general principle, whether there is co-operation of all the healing guides to help a patient if necessary."

Silver Birch replied: "The hall-mark of an evolved soul is that he will not deny anybody. We will help wherever we can. This is the standard set in the highest realms. Never refuse, my son, never turn away a soul. You have produced mental and spiritual effects that are eternal in their nature. Do not attempt to judge. You cannot see with the eyes of the spirit, and you cannot realise the measure of the work that is done.

"You help far more than you know. Be assured that the service that you render is one of the greatest services that can be performed in your world. Where it would seem that physical success has not crowned your efforts, do not despair; it is no reflection on you or those associated with you. The natural law must always work. You know there are no miracles; all is regulated by infinite love and infinite wisdom.

"I would say this to you and your collaborators. Try as much as you can to fix your gaze on the golden gleam of the spirit. Do not let earthly conditions disturb you. There are no difficulties that have crossed you path, or that will cross your path, which will be insuperable obstacles to the work to which you have set your hands, as long as the desire to serve is the paramount consideration. All will be overcome and the path of service will broaden as long as you desire to follow it. Not only do relief and ease and freedom follow in your trail, but you leave behind an incentive for others to aspire to the height that you have attained and which should provide you with the incentive to climb even to greater heights. We have not yet reached the apex of spiritual attainment. We are still far, far away, because the power of the spirit is like the Great Spirit, infinite in all its possibilities."

A member of the circle asked, "Is it a good thing for a person to go only to one healer?"

Silver Birch said: "Generally, the question is very hard to answer, because one would have to see the spiritual condition of the person and the spiritual condition surrounding the healer. You must remember there is a great range. There are some who heal not with any power of the spirit at all. They heal by a transmission of their own abundant, vital energy. The world of spirit is not involved in any way. That is not a bad thing, it is merely one form of healing. It is impossible to lay down any law as to what an individual should do. What is not a good thing to do is for an individual to make the whole round of healers because he gives nobody a chance. We would try to co-operate from our world, but this is setting up a flurry, an emotional flurry, round that individual that makes it harder for the power of the spirit to work. As you well know, spirit power is transmitted best in an atmosphere of passive quiescence, where in quietness the soul is able to come into its own."

Edwards said, "My question was that a person may be receiving direct healing from one and absent healing from another healer."

Silver Birch said: "But there is no conflict. You have proved that case. You have given healing to those who have had healing from others."

Here, George Burton interposed: "I often think of the journey of one's prayers in the spirit world. There are so many different ways people can pray, especially for healing. I know there are some who think that by concentrating for a long time on a person that much more help can be given. I would like to know how prayers reach the spirit world."

Silver Birch responded: "The answer to the question depends on the prayer and the one who prays. You appreciate that all is regulated by law in the whole realm of the universe; there is no chance and no miracle. If the prayer is merely a request of a selfish nature, it is an indication of the state of evolution which the individual has reached, and it is obvious that the prayer cannot produce any real effect. If the prayer is one that is unselfish, and has as its primary motive the desire to serve, that is an indication of the spiritual nature of the individual. By virtue of his evolution, he has already given wings to that prayer and it possesses a potency that is the direct result of his own spiritual attainment. Such a prayer automatically creates the conditions which will bring response. It is all controlled by the stage in evolution which the individual has reached."

A member of the circle said, "In other words, our prayers are no better than we are ourselves."

The guide declared, "That must be so."

Edwards said, "The simple prayer from a simple soul is of more value than a pretentious prayer from an archbishop."

Silver Birch answered: "It does not matter what the office

is, it is the soul that is important; it is the soul that provides the index. If the archbishop is a man of great spiritual attainment, then the prayer will be a potent one, but if he is one who is overloaded with theology, then the power of the spirit cannot penetrate. And the mass petitions of days of prayer, these are comparatively of no value either. The Great Spirit is not impressed with numbers, or with rank or title; it is the state of the soul that determines what happens.

"True prayer is a spiritual exercise in which the soul strives to soar higher than it has reached before. A prayer that desires to uplift and to serve is the prayer that will produce results. All your problems are known to the Great Spirit, who by the very nature of being the Great Spirit is familiar with all that takes place in the universe. The Great Spirit is the intelligence behind the natural law. Thus you cannot cheat the law; you cannot cheat the Great Spirit. You cannot even cheat yourself."

Olive Burton said: "Reverting to healing, some people hold the view that it is essential for the patient to have faith to be helped, but many believe that faith does not enter into it. What do you say?"

Silver Birch replied: "On the subject of healing, or in any exercise where the power of the spirit is involved, there are complex processes. It is not easy to answer a question with a simple Yes or No. There are cases where faith will help. Faith founded on knowledge will stimulate the spirit because it is a yearning of the spirit to find itself—not a blind faith, a credulous faith, not faith desiring miracles, but faith built on knowledge of natural spiritual laws. But even so where there is no faith, indeed, where there is complete ignorance, healing can still be achieved if individuals have reached the stage in evolution which determines that help is forthcoming."

Olive Burton asked, "We sometimes wonder why a person, who is obviously a sceptic, is helped and another, a good soul, does not get help."

The guide answered: "The line is drawn by the soul. You

must remember that your judgment is an outward one, not an inward one. You cannot see the soul, you are unable to determine the measure of its accomplishment. It is the soul that regulates the result. I lived in your world of matter a long time ago, I have lived in the world of spirit for a long time and I have seen the operation of many natural laws. I marvel at their mathematical exactitude; they never fail in their operation. There is true justice for every soul, not necessarily in your world, but in ours. When the ledger is drawn up, perfect justice is revealed.

"Do your task with willingness, with gladness, with service, and leave the result to the Great Spirit. You can do no more. It is not for you to determine who shall or who shall not be helped; you cannot do that, much as you would desire it. You cannot make the choice; you are instruments, as we are instruments of higher powers. Rest content that this superior wisdom and greater knowledge of the law will determine that each soul receives according to its need."

The subject of healing was again discussed on another occasion when a visitor from Pakistan put this question to Silver Birch, "In view of the wonderful cures one so frequently hears about, why is it that some people with apparently small ailments seem to be incurable?"

The guide answered: "There is nothing incurable, for every disease has a cure. The universe is simple but complex; there are depths of profundity, there are laws within laws. Knowledge leads to knowledge and knowledge leads to further knowledge. There is no finality to understanding. Wisdom is infinite. I say all this because you must try to realise that there is no easy answer to questions which touch upon the very nature of the soul, its constitution, its origin, its evolution and its destiny.

"Again and again I hear people of your world say: 'Why is this one healed and another one not healed? Why is it that even when there is love and the desire to heal, the cure is not forthcoming, yet when there is no love and a comparative stranger presents himself the cure is effected?' These matters are regulated by law; the law which determines all this is the law relating to the soul's state of evolution, and that is not only fixed by the episodes of this life, but often they take cognisance of the events of former lives. You cannot judge the things of the spirit by measuring them with earthly standards. If you attempt to reduce the whole of life to a physical explanation you will fail, but alas, unfortunately, too often encased in matter yourself you cannot see with the eyes of the spirit and so there are apparent injustices and inequalities.

"The Great Spirit is perfect justice, the Great Spirit is perfect wisdom because the Great Spirit is perfect law in operation. It is not possible for you to attain to the summits of all the knowledge there is because your understanding is limited to finite measurements. Do not accept the idea that there are any incurable cases; there are not. What is true sometimes is that the soul has not earned the right for that palliation, easement, relief of cure and that in effect what is happening is the law of Karma in operation. This is not said to encourage any ideas of fatalism, but to establish the principle that law is always in operation, even if you cannot see it."

'The architect of all life'

MANY thousands appreciated Silver Birch's prayers. When at a sitting he was asked why he used the "antiquated language of the English Bible" he answered:

"I am an old soul and I like the old language best. I think it has more beauty. When you are striving to reach the highest that you know, then you find that in an atmosphere of beauty you obtain more peace.

"The soul, because it is part of the Great Spirit, is filled with its beauty. In striving to express itself in earthly language it seeks those sentiments more appropriate to its true self. And they, I consider, are best expressed in that simple but majestic language in which some of the Bible was written."

Silver Birch opened his circle, using "antiquated" language, saying:

"Oh Great White Spirit, Thou art the architect of all life no matter what form it may take, for Thine is the infinite law which is responsible for its existence. Thine is the plan which has conceived every phase of universal activity and Thy love broods over all.

"Throughout the universe, in which there are myriads of manifestations of life, Thy law takes cognisance of them all. Thou hast provided all that is necessary for their sustenance, for their maintenance and upkeep. Thou hast provided the means by which all is able to move in one concerted whole, each aspect forming part of a vast harmonious pattern which is the result of Thy execution.

"We pay tribute to the unchanging, immutable, omnipotent law, for we know that there is no circumstance in life which is outside the scope of its governance. We desire to spread greater knowledge of its existence among all Thy children, so that understanding it, they may see more clearly the purpose of their being, their relationship to Thee and know what it is they have to do to fulfil their part in the divine scheme.

"We desire also to reveal the existence of Thy spirit within them, that dynamic wellspring of divinity which is responsible for all their consciousness, for their breathing and thinking, for their life and for all that is real about them.

"Once they knew the depths which Thou hast placed within them and understood the tie, the divine tie, by which they are bound to Thee, they could release a flood of power which, surging through their beings, would enable a greater manifestation of Thee to take place.

"Thus there would come into being more of the gifts of the spirit and a brighter illumination would flood their lives and help to clear away the darkness that obscures so many from seeing the truth which is available to them.

"We pray to be of service to all who need it, to bring them to those paths of knowledge and understanding where they can find the solution of all their problems, the strength that will guide them in their hours of weakness and perplexity, so that they, too, may know that Thou art always with them.

"This is the prayer of Thy Indian servant who seeks to serve."

Chapter 2

'WHEN KNOWLEDGE REIGNS'

OVER the years many and varied were those who travelled to Maurice Barbanell's NW London flat to hear his guide speak. Some came from overseas, the visit to Hannen Swaffer's home circle being a highlight of their trip. Others were from nearer home.

Such was the case when John, an eleven-year-old lad, went one night to meet and question Silver Birch. Even at his tender age he accepted Spiritualism and all it stands for quite naturally. When his father passed on, young John accepted without question that he had gone to the spirit world to join his sister.

The guide began by telling him of the presence of these two relatives, who were as excited as he was. "I never knew my sister," said John.

"But she knows you," the guide replied.

"I expect she only saw me when I was a baby."

The guide said: "No, she has seen you grow up from a little baby to the strapping giant that you now are. You must remember that although you cannot see her she can see you. She has quite a different pair of eyes from yours, because her eyes can see right through walls and doors."

"Yes, I know, mortal walls," was John's calm reply.

"She can see even though she has not got your eyes. She sees with her soul. And when you see with your soul, then you can see a very, very long way, hundreds of thousands of miles."

"How old is my sister now in spirit life?" asked the boy.

Silver Birch said: "That is a very difficult question. Let me explain it to you. We do not grow old like you do. We do not have birthdays like you do. We do not say that we are now one year older or two years older. We do not grow in that way at all. We grow spiritually, that is, we grow towards perfection."

"What is perfection?" asked John.

The guide replied: "Perfection is the final state when all things come into their own and there are no flaws, no weaknesses, no faults at all. That is perfection."

The boy said, "In other words peace."

Silver Birch answered: "Yes, when you have perfection you have peace, because you have perfect peace. But perfection is not something that you attain, because it is part of an infinite process. It is always going on; it never comes to an end."

"But you come to an end when you get to it," John said.

"You never get to it, it always goes on. You cannot imagine that, can you? But it is so. There is no beginning and no end to the things of the spirit. They have always been in some form. It is a constant process of getting better all the time. Your sister has not grown, as you understand growth; she has grown in beauty of mind and spirit. She has matured, she has unfolded, she has developed, but not physically. I can only tell you how old she is according to the way you count time. What I want to make you realise is something that you know in part, that she and your father are always with you. This is a great secret that many people have not got; that all the time they are with you because they love and want to help you. If you tell people, they won't believe that, will they? They think if they cannot see anything there is nothing there. There is a lot of sorrow in the world owing to the fact that they do not understand it. If they did, they would not weep when death comes, because death is not a tragedy. It is for those left behind sometimes, but not for those who experience it. For them it is another birthday. They have evolved into a new life altogether. Try and remember that, John. You know about your sister because you have seen her, haven't you?"

John said: "I want to see her with these eyes."

"If you close them sometimes you will see her," the guide told him.

"Just like I see everybody in this room?" the boy inquired.

Silver Birch answered: "Not quite the same way. It is the sight of the soul again. If you want to see anything that belongs to the spirit you cannot see it with the eyes; neither if you want to hear them do you hear with the ears."

The guide added: "Your father is pleased with you. He says so. He ought to know. He is looking after you and is going to guide you and see that your feet will go on the right path."

"Thank him for me, will you?"

"He hears you, you know. It is hard to understand that, isn't it, John? But every time you speak, or even think, he knows. It comes to him as a flash."

"What sort of flash?"

"Every time you think, your thought has a little light."

John asked: "What sort of light, a mortal light? I know we cannot see it. Is it like looking at the flash of a match?"

The guide's answer was: "Oh no, it is a little coloured light. It is just like the flame of a candle, but it has many colours. Every thought has a different colour according to the nature of the thought. That is how we see these thoughts when they come to us. When we look at you we see you as a colour. You are a mass of colour all the time. Each of these colours, to those who are trained, mean something, so that you cannot have any secrets from us. All the colours show us what you think, what you desire and everything about you."

John asked: "What is the point of learning about Spiritualism?"

Silver Birch answered: "All knowledge is important. You

are always better off if you have knowledge rather than ignorance. Where you have ignorance, you walk in the darkness; where you have knowledge you walk in the light. Which would you rather do?"

"Walk in the light," replied the lad.

"Then you must have knowledge. Knowledge is the most precious possession, because with knowledge you have wisdom, with knowledge, you have reason, with knowledge you have judgement, but without knowledge you are not properly equipped, are you? Here is a world in which you live. You may think it is a very big world, but it is only a small part of the universe. The reason you are put into this world is to gain as much knowledge as you can, so that you are ready for the next stage of your life.

"And when it comes to what is called Spiritualism, it is very important to understand what the purpose of life is, because unless you understand what the purpose of life is, well, you do not know what it is all about, do you? Your mother is better off now because she has knowledge about your father and sister than when she had no knowledge, isn't she?"

"Yes, she gets more help," said John.

"Well, that is the answer to the question, isn't it? What next?"

John asked, "What do the spirit people think of the inventing department of the world, whether the atomic bomb is both good and bad?"

Silver Birch said: "That is a very big question, isn't it? I tell you what I think. I cannot tell you what everyone thinks here. I think this is a clear example of the value of knowledge rather than ignorance. Because of the war, scientists in your world were spurred on to make researches and experiments, with the result that they have found a secret, atomic energy, that was used in the release of a bomb. They have found this secret many, many years before they were mentally and spiritually ready to deal with it. If this secret had been found in another hundred or two hundred years' time, it might well be that the people of your world would have advanced so much that they would know what to do with the secret when they found it. Now they do not know, because here is a secret that could be used to help or harm. The only answer to that question depends on the mental and spiritual make-up of the people of this world. Do you follow that?"

John said, "Not the last bit."

The guide told him: "Let me try to put it another way. This is a discovery which is in advance of its time. The people of your world, generally speaking, are not ready for the discovery that they have made and so it has been used for destruction. If they were ready for it, they would have used it for helpful purposes. Now we go back to your first question. If all scientists were people who had knowledge, knowledge of spiritual things, then they would not be worried about this question at all. They would know the answer, because, being spiritually ready, they would know the value of the invention and its application would be only for human good."

John showed his grasp of the answer by saying, "If they knew what it really was, they would use it the right way."

Silver Birch said, "Yes, it is only because they have not had the spiritual understanding that they are faced with this problem of what to do with this invention."

John's next question was, "What is the difference between a ghost and a spirit?"

The guide replied: "That is a very good question. A ghost is a spirit, but a spirit need not be a ghost. What you call a ghost can be a spirit bound to earth because of the very poor sort of life he has lived, or else reflections left behind by the concentrated hatred or evil of someone who has lived in a certain place. What is called a ghost is usually the first kind, that is, a spirit who is nearer to earth than he is to the spirit world, because although he has died his life, his selfish life, will chain him to the earth."

"I have not really got any more questions," said John.

"How will you mark my paper for this examination?" asked the guide.

"I don't know the answers myself."

Said Silver Birch: "You would not know whether I was giving you the right answers or not. Good! That is satisfactory, anyway. The great thing to remember always is this, that in addition to the love that surrounds you on earth, there is a great love that surrounds you from our world. Even if you cannot see it, it is there. Even if you cannot feel it, it is there. When you are in trouble, just stop, send us a thought, send your father a thought, send your sister a thought, and they will help you and guide you as to what to do."

The implications of the atomic bomb were discussed at another seance when this question was put to Silver Birch, "How do you think it best that nations and mankind can repel the fear which is automatically created by the atomic bomb?"

The guide replied: "The root of the whole trouble is that at the control of human affairs are not the laws of spirit and their application, but fear and greed, envy and selfishness and the lust for power. There is, unfortunately, not the desire amongst all to serve one another, to live in harmony and peace, but to aggrandise one nation above the other, to enrich one class at the expense of the other. The systems that still rule are founded on the philosophy of materialism, even though the name may have been, to some extent, abandoned. People declare that wealth and rank and colour take pride of place. They try to fashion their systems upon these physical foundations; they ignore the eternal realities. They attempt to judge the whole of life by that small fraction of it which is seen and heard and touched and tasted, in fact, just that infinitesimal fragment which is cognised by the physical senses.

"But life is greater than matter and man is more than clay and dust. Life is not to be understood in terms of chemistry or medicine or atoms. The riddle of life is not solved in the laboratories of science; neither can the soul be found with a scalpel nor analysed by any chemical means. Life eludes all attempts at material explanation. And yet, throughout the whole world of matter, the majority of mankind live in complete divorce from the eternal, spiritual realities. The majority of mankind attempt to ignore the vital facts, the facts which make all life possible. The whole of your world exists because of spirit, and you yourself owe your existence to spirit.

"Reality is not to be found in matter, neither is it to be discovered within your bodily frame. The seed of existence is not to be located within any bodily organ. You are spiritual beings now. You do not attain spiritual natures by coming to our world. From the moment of conception you are spiritual beings and there is nothing that you can do to cut yourselves off from that reality which enables you to live. The whole of your world exists because of spirit. Without spirit there is no life, for life is spirit and spirit is life.

"It is the essential part of our task to teach to mankind these truths which can be demonstrated in such a fashion that they must become acceptable to those who will listen, unless, of course, they are so blind that they will not believe, though one rose from the dead. Until the recognition of the fact of man's spiritual nature plays a predominant part in all human affairs, there will be fear. Today it is an atomic bomb, tomorrow it will be something even more awesome and stupendous. The long course of history shows very clearly that attempts to rule by force and tyranny must fail. Dictatorships have come, have thrived and have vanished. Tyrants do not for ever dwell on their thrones. The spirit of man being supreme and divine insists, albeit falteringly at first, on claiming its heritage. Freedom cannot be enslaved for ever, neither can liberty be imprisoned for all time. These are the qualities of the spirit which must endure. Man does not live by bread alone. He is more than a physical being. He is a mind and a soul. He is a spirit, an integral part of that same spirit which fashioned every phase of life in a multitudinous universe whose bounds no man can set.

"And when these truths dwell in their rightful place, all fear and anxiety will have vanished. The children of the Great Spirit will not walk, day by day, with anguish in their hearts, with fear in their minds, with bent backs wondering always what the morrow will bring forth. They will have claimed their spiritual birthright because man is a spirit who must live in the sunlight of freedom. His spirit must find full expression. The spirit which is eternal cannot be cramped and confined and restricted. It will burst its bonds, destroying all the opposition which compels it to live in the darkness. When knowledge reigns and ignorance has fled, fear will not be the activating motive. To answer your question, we must spread knowledge, for when all have the knowledge some will have the responsibility that knowledge brings. Regeneration, a change of heart, the application of spiritual values, these are the only means by which peace will come to a troubled world."

Later, Silver Birch added: "In times of stress and difficulty it behoves all those who have the knowledge to act as ambassadors of truth. It is a sad commentary when you find that those whose lives have been enriched with knowledge, and who have been given comfort in their hour of sorrow, fail to see the implications of that which has come to them. The gift of mediumship is a sacred one; it is an office which should not be lightly held. And yet, unfortunately, it cannot be said that all mediums, even the majority of them, regard their gifts as being divine in origin and seek to use them unselfishly in the service of the suffering, the weak and the needy.

"And among those to whom the truth has been revealed, sometimes as a blinding flash, illuminating the darkness which has surrounded them for long, even there selfishness too often rules and service is forgotten. There is much cleansing to be done, much purifying, much regeneration.

To those to whom is entrusted the task of spreading truth, let them look within themselves and see whether they are not called upon to rededicate their lives to the vision which has too often lost some of its pristine glory, to the rich outlook which has become tarnished with the passage of time. Let them stir themselves to use their lives as instruments of that greater power which desires that it shall be made more manifest in your world."

'So many live in the shadows'

OH Great White Spirit, who can measure Thy infinitude of love, who can describe Thy divine beneficence, or give an adequate representation of Thy majesty?

Thou art beyond all finite understanding, beyond all limitation and restriction. Thou art the infinite spirit, the source of all that has ever been and will ever be.

Thine is the spirit that has made love possible and endowed all consciousness with the attributes of Thy divinity.

It is Thy spirit stirring within man which enables him to rise to heights of idealism, self-sacrifice and service. It is Thy spirit which distinguishes him from all other forms of creation.

Thou art manifest within him and he is the Great Spirit in microscopic form.

We desire to make all Thy children fully aware of all the properties and attributes and faculties of the spirit. Without a knowledge of them they dwell in ignorance. They are unarmed in the battle of life.

But with knowledge of what they are, they are fully equipped and are able to derive from life the joy, the beauty, the sweetness, the fullness and the radiance which can be theirs.

So many live in the shadows cast by reality when they

could be living in the sunlight itself. So many are subjected to difficulties, to storms within, because they lack the understanding which will bring them stability, poise and confidence.

It is this knowledge of spiritual realities that we desire to offer the world of matter, so that all who dwell in it may understand themselves, may know of the links that unite them to Thee and to one another, may realise that the bonds of love are not severed by death and that affection and kinship continue beyond the grave.

It is part of our mission, to which we have dedicated ourselves, to disseminate truth as widely as possible, so that all may live armed with knowledge, guided by reason and with the understanding of the eternal power of which they are an integral part.

Chapter 3

'THE LIGHT AND THE SHADE'

TRAGEDY came into the life of film star Merle Oberon when the aeroplane carrying her fiancé crashed in flames a few seconds after he had bidden her good-bye. Naturally, for a time, she was stunned by the blow. She wondered whether Spiritualism could help her. Then Miss Oberon came across Hannen Swaffer's book on Spiritualism, *My Greatest Story*, and was moved when she read a quotation from the teachings of Silver Birch. One extract of the guide's teachings made a great appeal to her.

When she met Swaffer, she asked if she could talk to Silver Birch. The guide agreed. A few days after the air crash she visited his circle. In addition, Miss Oberon sat with other mediums. As a result of a short inquiry she became satisfied with the evidence of her fiancé's survival. This evidence changed her from a grief-stricken woman into one whose confidence had been restored by psychic knowledge.

Miss Oberon was brought to the seance room by Swaffer, who said to Silver Birch: "As you know, I expect, she has been through a great tragedy. Although she is bearing up with extraordinary courage, she seeks guidance."

Silver Birch said to the film star: "You are very brave, but knowledge will help you. Try to appreciate that it is only through sorrow and suffering, which are the testing times of the soul, that you can acquire the greatest knowledge and the greatest understanding. Life, both here and what you call hereafter, cannot be pursued on one plane alone, a plane of unsullied joy. There must come the light and the shade. It is only because of darkness that you know light. If there were no darkness, there would be no light, for all would be darkness or light and it would be the same thing. It is only through difficulty and sorrow that the soul comes into its own. This is not easy, it is hard, but it is part of your eternal equipment, because the whole of your purpose on earth is to acquire that character and that spiritual growth and attainment which will enable you to face the next stage of life that awaits you.

"Your path has not been an easy one in life. You have had ups and downs. And when it seemed that the cup of happiness was offered to you, it was bitterly dashed away. Now you will not be satisfied until you are assured beyond any doubt that life and love continue or whether they come to an end. You have garnered sufficient to realise that they do not come to an end, but you are not yet in the possession of all the facts which will give you the assurance that you require. Am I correct?"

"Yes," was the film star's reply.

"Try to realise—and this is how best I can help you—that all of us in life are spiritual beings first and foremost. That is why we live, for the spirit is the mainspring of existence. All that lives, breathes, moves and has consciousness does so because it is spirit. Spirit is what you call God and I call the Great Spirit. This spirit, which is that portion of God, the Great Spirit, is incarnated into matter so that it can obtain the experiences to fit it for its next stage of evolution, just like the child going to school to learn the lessons to fit it for the world beyond school. Now you, like everybody else, are a spiritual being. The things of matter will tarnish and fade away, the things of the spirit are eternal; they will persist for all time. That which is founded on matter cannot endure, for matter is but the shell, the husk; it is not the reality. Most people in your world are worshipping illusion; they are pursuing will-o'-the-wisps; they have not found reality; it has eluded them; they have not found themselves.

"If you can see life as part of a cosmic purpose, a plan, a scheme by a Great Spirit actuated by love and beneficence, and understand that you are part, an irrefragable part, of that scheme, then even when you cannot understand the experiences that befall you, you will realise that they are still part of the eternal scheme. Anything which is part of the spirit cannot die. Death is not extinction; death is merely the means by which the spirit is released to carry on elsewhere. It is the antithesis of birth—birth, the means by which the spirit makes its entrance and death, the means by which it makes its exit. But you, you are not your body, you are not your head, eyes, nose, limbs, muscles or your chemical assembly; that is not you. All these are merely the means by which you, the spirit, express yourself in a physical world. But apart from the physical world you continue to exist.

"When death occurs, the spirit takes with it everything that belongs to the individual, everything which makes that individual different from every other individual. The consciousness, mind, traits, habits, idiosyncrasies, the power to love, to inspire and give affection, friendship, fellowship— all these are spiritual qualities and because of that they persist. All that is the real you cannot die, and all that which belongs to the real you cannot die either. Whether you can realise this or not, and it is difficult to grasp in its fullness, all that you love and that loves you is still alive. Does that help you?"

"Yes," came the answer.

"Try to forget the picture of material things because they are not the reality," added the guide. "The reality does not lie in physical things."

"Is my fiancé there now?" asked Miss Oberon.

"Yes," said the guide. "He tried to speak through the medium to you at your last meeting, but, of course, it is not an easy task. It takes quite a good deal of work to make it perfect, but if you persist he will succeed. You realise, of course, that he is very emotional, and it is not an easy task because this passing was not an expected one—far from it."

"What is he doing now?" asked Miss Oberon. "Where is he? Is he all right?"

Turning to Swaffer, the guide said: "This is a big shock for two people, one in your world and one in mine. Adjustment has not yet taken place. It cannot be expected that it should be otherwise."

Then speaking to Miss Oberon the guide said: "I will help you best if I try to explain that this young man is close to you. He is not doing anything. He is standing with you. He has to learn all the processes of communication, not only in the sense of the control of a medium, but also in the other aspect of making his thoughts and his desires and wishes known to you, which is the equivalent to a great engineering feat. He will not go away from you until he has completely mastered this.

"Once you can achieve inner tranquillity, you will find unmistakably that you are getting from him the help and guidance that he desires to give and you desire to receive. Try to appreciate that you are dealing with very sensitive and delicate vibrations which are easily disturbed by your thoughts. If you radiate an atmosphere of anxiety and shock and sorrow, you surround yourself with heaviness, a denseness that forms a handicap to communication. If you can achieve—and this is not easy—serenity, if you can radiate tranquillity, if you can have inner peace, these provide the best conditions for results from our world. We cannot work when the atmosphere is charged with conflicting emotions. We can work best when there is a receptivity, a passiveness, so that we can reach you."

After some personal messages, the guide said: "What you may find difficult to understand is that he is closer to you than he is to me, even although he is in my world and not in yours. Do you understand that? It is the earth which attracts him, not the spirit. One of the difficulties is that he knew nothing about this subject. It did not come within his purview. He is very glad because you have helped him more than you know by coming to meet him in this fashion. Too many people regard death as a finality and those who have gone from their side linger only in memories and not in actualities. But you have helped him by presenting him with an opportunity to get closer to you and not by creating a wall around yourself. For that he is very grateful."

"Was his passing painful?" asked Miss Oberon.

"No, he did not feel anything," said the guide. "It was too quick. Have you not been told that?"

"Yes."

"It was over in a flash," the guide stated.

"That is what she was told," Swaffer interposed.

"Yes, it was very quick and there was a long period of rest for that reason," Silver Birch told her.

"How long?" she asked.

The guide replied: "It is very difficult to answer such a question because we have no measurement of time like you have. But it is longer than the usual period for those who have to adjust themselves. All violent passings produce a shock. It is not a permanent shock, but it is a shock, because the spirit should not leave its body precipitated in this fashion, and this requires adjustments to be made."

After receiving some further personal messages, Miss Oberon asked: "Is he happy now? Is he all right?"

Silver Birch said: "He is not happy because he does not want to be here. He wants to be with you in your world. You will have to help him and he will have to help himself. That is a temporary condition, but he is quite all right. There is nothing that can harm his spirit, and soon he will adjust himself.

"The Great Spirit, who made the universe, is filled with love. You must trust that power which fashioned each one of us and know that all will be explained. All that you cannot understand now will become clearer on another occasion. I do not say this to fob you off, but it is so. You are looking at life through eyes of matter and eternity cannot be appreciated only with earthly scales. True perspective will come later on, but the things that matter, life, love, identity, all these continue. Death has no power over life or love."

Pointing to a member of the circle, Silver Birch said: "Her father is in our world. He has been here for many months now. He has become accustomed to it. Now it is so natural to him that he sits in his old chair by the family table, refusing to allow his transition from one sphere to another to make any difference to his love or his life. He is calm, not troubled. He has adjusted himself; he is closer than he has ever been before. Those who remain behind feel him, know he is there, for they have unfolded a faculty of the soul which gives them the perception that hitherto was lacking. The Great Spirit is guided by love, and there is compensation in all things."

Finally, Silver Birch told Miss Oberon of the spirit presence of her mother, saying that she had made way for the fiancé because she felt that all the time should be given to him. "Your mother is a very sweet and radiant soul who has helped you far more than you know," he said. "Have I helped you at all?"

"Yes, thank you," was her reply.

"Do not thank me, thank the Great Spirit," said Silver Birch. "We are all His ministers striving to do His will. Go on seeking for knowledge. It is true; those who seek do find; to those who knock the door is opened; and those who ask do receive."

An old Spiritualist, whose life, he declared, had been spirit guided in England and abroad, was another to be invited to the circle. Silver Birch greeted him as "one who is not a stranger to the truths of the spirit, who has travelled the path and has reached a stage of awareness where much is being revealed."

"It is a long road that you have travelled, a road where the milestones marked many decisive stages," the guide continued, "but you know that you are guided by love that seeks to use you in the great plan. Now you can look back and see that even what appeared to be very dark shadows were essential elements in the great plan. It was only by following implicitly the promptings of the spirit that you could fulfil the role that you must play.

"The task you are to perform before you lay down your physical body is a significant one. Much has been revealed to you, stage by stage. There is much more to be done; you have caught glimpses; the full light, the complete illumination, has not yet descended on you. This requires slow development and spiritual progress before it can be yours. Do you understand me?"

"I do," came the reply.

"You have asked yourself many times, 'What is the purpose of all this?'"

"I feel that there is a purpose," the visitor replied. "I have not questioned the purpose. I am particularly anxious to see a little light that will illumine the path a little further."

The guide added: "You are an old soul. This is not the first time you have trod this path. Do you know that?"

"I have had awareness of something in that respect," was the answer, "but it conflicts with certain other ideas that I have which I will not touch on at the moment."

"I know about your conflict," Silver Birch told him. "That can easily be resolved. It is the conflict between this aspect of consciousness, which is functioning in your present existence, and the larger aspect which is part of your larger existence. In certain states, when you have withdrawn yourself from the world and, as the Bible says, you have been filled with the power of the spirit, your soul has come into its own, and you have felt that touch with the larger self as it has clamoured for recognition, beating in on the senses of your body.

"As to the purpose, it is the great purpose that activates and motivates all those who return from our world and who belong to those groups dedicated to the task of serving mankind. It is to cast the bread of knowledge upon the sea of ignorance—that is the purpose. To hold the light so that souls in darkness can see its rays, to indicate a haven and sanctuary for those who have lost their way, for the troubled in mind and spirit who seek peace. It is a great purpose which unites us all and makes us one. It is a purpose that is greater than all the differences of body, race, nationality or religion. You have your special part to play in this plan, and you have helped many."

"I am very grateful to you for explaining the matter as you have," said the Spiritualist.

"There are two problems that confront us," the guide continued. "One is to awaken slumbering souls to the task they have to perform, the other is to hold in check those who are awakened, for they desire to rush when the power of the spirit must discipline itself according to the laws which make its flow possible. The Great Spirit is not in a hurry. The universe will not disappear; the laws will not change. Be patient and know that what has been revealed to you is an indication of what is still to be revealed to you, and have perfect faith that the love which guides you will not fail you if you are prepared to serve with a full heart."

Here the visitor commented: "I am grateful for the wisdom that has guided me, for the noble souls who are my guides and beloved friends. I hope that that association between us will in no way be severed through any fault of my own."

The Spiritualist had prepared for the sitting by framing three questions, the first being:

"Man, I believe, is the highest work of Omnipotence, the Creator of the universe, and as such he, in his physical and organic structure, is a microcosmic manifestation of the macrocosm, each formed and functioning without differentiation. Yet what is it that determines and effects the apparent separate personalities of individuals, the numberless types of countenances, expressions, emotions, tendencies, identifiable and recordable differences in each being, embracing degrees of intelligence, mannerisms, voice, aptitude, capacity, etc?"

"That is quite a question," said Silver Birch. "Do not confuse matter with spirit, or matter with mind. Man is a triune being obeying the natural laws of the universe. His body obeys the physical laws, his mind the mental laws, his spirit the spiritual laws, and all these work in concert with one another. Thus you have laws within laws within laws, sometimes seemingly contradictory, but not in reality, when you have the key which unlocks the riddle.

"Not only are there laws within laws, but each aspect of man's being mingles and merges with other aspects so that there is a constant interplay of the mental, spiritual and physical forces. There is no sharp dividing line between the three aspects of being. The body is obeying the physical law of heredity. The mind is the expression of the spirit as conditioned by the physical brain and the other physical senses. The expression of spirit in matter is limited by the matter through which it can express itself. Thus there are infinite numbers of variations and permutations of expressions because the spirit is affecting the body and the body is affecting the spirit so far as its expression is concerned. Does that make it clear?"

"To some extent it does," was the response. "That will help me very much indeed. May I ask the second question? Since I believe that man is outborn from his source, the source of all life, are you able to help me to understand and know what are the stages, and their nature, in the transition of individual man from his origin to his lowest plane of matter, from which I assume that the soul, at the time of its separation from the physical body, ascends in progressive stages through the spheres to ultimate reunion with the

Infinite? And, if this is so, can you tell me what are the stages and the nature of man's progression hereafter?"

"That, too, is quite a question," Silver Birch commented. "No, I cannot. I cannot express the whole of spiritual life in language which is restricted for its understanding to material events. There is no language capable of explaining fully the infinity of spiritual life, but, very briefly, man is a spirit, though the Great Spirit is not a man.

"The Great Spirit is the primal source of all existence; the Great Spirit is the cause, the supreme architect, the king of kings. Spirit is life and life is spirit. Man, as spirit, has always existed. Man, as individual spirit, starts his existence with earthly incarnation, so far as this plane of life is concerned. The purpose of matter is to provide the individual vehicle for spirit, and the reason for earthly existence is to help that individuality to unfold.

"Death, which is birth into the spirit of life, is the means by which the individuated spirit takes on the second stage of its pilgrimage, that is, to develop, quicken, unfold and to perfect all the innate qualities of spirit, so as to draw closer to the source of all being. Man, being spirit, is potentially perfect as the Great Spirit is perfect. But I do not think that reunion is achieved in the sense that man is absorbed into the Godhead. Rather do I assert that the processes of development and perfection are as infinite as the Great Spirit is."

"I follow that and I am grateful," said the visitor. "What you have said on the second question somewhat explains the third. Is reincarnation, as expounded by its propagandists, a fact in the operation of the fundamental law governing the destiny of the soul of the individual man? If not, are the individual characteristics and peculiarities in each human being accumulated inheritances from previous births in other states or planes anterior to this, in the course of his descent to earth and prior to transitory incarnation on this lowest plane, from which he ascends on another or opposite path, his progression accelerated or retarded according to his experiences and accumulations in all stages of his being? I hope I have made that clear."

"It is not easy to answer in a few sentences questions touching the profundity of existence," said the spirit guide. "First I must say that I am not clear as to what the propagandists of reincarnation say, but speaking for myself, and after all, I have no authority to speak for any other, I assert that reincarnation is a fact. I have no quarrel with those who disagree with me. I have seen individuals who have previously incarnated into matter. It is done by those who have specific missions to perform, a voluntary act in order to redeem a pledge.

"What incarnates is another aspect of the same individuality, and I do not mean personality. If you visualise man as an individual, who in his earthly life is like an iceberg in which you have one small portion manifesting and the larger portion not manifesting, then that is the end of one incarnation. In a successive incarnation, a portion of the submerged self will come into the world of matter, two different personalities, but one individual. And in spirit life, as progression takes place, it is part of the submerged self that comes to the surface all the time. Do not attempt to understand all that is in reincarnation, or judge it with the eyes of matter, but try to see it with the reason that comes from the knowledge of the spirit, and that answers the question."

"It does indeed answer it," was the comment.

A visitor from abroad, for many years a great admirer of Silver Birch, asked the guide: "One frequently hears of the necessity for some board of control to test and pass mediums for public demonstrations. Such boards are liable to be a danger to free expression of beliefs. What is your opinion?"

"I would think that this is a case when the remedy could be worse than the disease," replied the guide.

"And who is going to examine the examiner?" exclaimed a member of the circle.

"My son, the spirit bloweth where it listeth," added Silver Birch. "No man can set aside the channels where the power of the spirit shall flow. The power of the spirit cannot be regimented; it cannot answer to dictation; it cannot be restricted; it cannot be confined to any instrument. Matter is the servant of spirit, it is not its master. Matter exists because of spirit, spirit does not exist because of matter. Matter is inferior; spirit is superior. Matter lives only because it is the reflection of spirit.

"None can say where spirit shall flow. It will flow wherever there are conditions enabling it to reach its object. As usually it is directed by love, human love, and sometimes divine love, there is none in your world who can decide where it shall be made manifest. And if all the boards existed, the power of the spirit will still flow according to its nature and its desire. I do not say this to support what is undoubtedly true, that there are many public exhibitions of psychic power which are unworthy because they display what is a very immature result. But that is vastly different from regimentation and control and dictatorship."

When Silver Birch greeted the visitor at the beginning of the seance, he said: "I am very happy to have you here, my son, and I am not unfamiliar with you, or your little lady. Many times you have sent a request out to me and I have heard you. I would like you to know that your footsteps are being guided and that there is a long way for you to go. There are difficulties that have come your way, but they are not insuperable. Just as in the past difficulties which have loomed and seemed to be insuperable have vanished, so these others will vanish too. You have not yet reached your true sanctuary. I know your heart and your desires, and they will be fulfilled. But you must be patient.

"Do not be in a hurry. It is usual for us to find those who awaken to knowledge of spiritual realities, after waiting some time to do so, are eager to press forward. The Great Spirit is not in a hurry and eternal processes work themselves out according to immutable law. Try to bring yourself into the harmony and rhythm of spiritual law. You are, forgive me saying it, impetuous by nature. There is much for you to do. The desire to serve is implanted in your breast and you will serve, my son, but the time has not yet come for this to happen.

"Keep your feet on the path. Let your heart sing with rejoicing that you have found the light. Know that this light will always lead you nearer to the centre of all light. You are fortunate because truth has come to you in comparatively early days. Be thankful for it, nurture it, encourage it to stay with you always, for as it stays it will increase its influence, and your mind being made receptive, still greater truth will come to you."

To another guest Silver Birch gave this advice. "Worry and anxiety are not good companions for the soul. You have been safely brought to where you are; you will be safely carried all the rest of the way. You must always know that and it is a hard lesson to learn. You must be able to say: 'I am part of the Great Spirit, indestructible, imperturbable. I face all that life brings me from day to day knowing that I have the power to overcome everything.' That is what you are here for, to learn that lesson. Face each day as a means of greater opportunity for unfoldment. The problems will always come and they will go. They tarry for a while, that is all. Love will help you to put them in their proper place."

Lastly the guide addressed another visitor whose father had passed on and who attached himself to Silver Birch's band of helpers: "It has not been easy to keep your father back all this time. I wish you had the eyes of the spirit. I, who it is said have some mastery in your language, feel its inadequacy when I try to tell you of the love that streams from him. I am conscious of the inability of words which, after all, are very poor symbols, to express the reality that exists where words cannot explain.

"It is not always so that this great love exists. There is love between those whom the ties of blood have brought into close relationship. Sometimes it reaches greater heights and greater depths. This is so in your case. It was not spoken of in your world, but in ours it is expressed in the very nature of all that emanates from us. You cannot see it and you cannot feel it, except perhaps a pale glimmer, yet it is there all the time, a force vital in intensity, a compelling dynamic force that is as real as life itself, for love is life. Life was built, life exists because of love.

"I say all this to try and convey what comes from your father. It is as if his soul were entwined in your own, for to him you are he and he is you. That is how he visualises you all the time. If you have fears at any time they would be foolish because there is nothing to fear whilst there is such love. If you, by virtue of your human weakness, stray sometimes from the path, as all humans must do, it is because you cannot realise that intensity of love that would keep you always there, where you should be. I do not hurt you by saying that. I understand earthly things very well."

"I understand you," said the son. "I know exactly what you are trying to tell me."

"The Great Spirit is love and love is the Great Spirit," went on the guide. "What your father expresses is something that is truly divine. It is his life that is poured out upon you. You may have problems; people in your world must have problems; that is why they are in your world. But there is nothing so big that this love cannot overcome. Son, go forward and know that this power that guides you is the power that gave you life, it cannot fail you. Beside that all other messages fall into insignificance. If I have conveyed that then your heart should be singing and your step should be light, for you would know that you are richly blessed."

'We pray for strength'

LET us attune ourselves to the highest that we can reach. Let us put on one side all thoughts of stress and anxiety. Let us dismiss all cares and enter into the silence, to be bathed in the benediction that comes from the inner realms.

Let us approach the power which fashioned all life and ask that everything which is said and done this evening shall resound to its glory and have the effect of bringing us closer to the power which we call the Great Spirit.

Oh, Great White Spirit, the whole of the universe pays tribute to the wonder and marvel of the natural laws which Thy infinite intelligence has conceived and Thy divine love sustains.

We recognise that Thou hast made provision for all that exists. Nothing is too small to be outside the orbit of Thy love and Thy watchfulness.

All Thy children, of many different hues, races and religions are imbued with Thy divinity which draws them together in an invisible but unbreakable bond of the spirit, making them for all eternity members of Thy divine family.

Within every child of the Great Spirit there are the means to unite them, to make them recognise their common heritage, so that in understanding it they could build systems which would outlaw war and chaos, bloodshed and misery, and enable them to dwell in peace, cultivating all the gifts, beauties and riches of their spiritual natures.

We pray for strength to be given to all those whose hearts, minds and spirits are dedicated to the great task of liberating humanity. We pray for greater strength and guidance for them all, that they may recognise that theirs is a noble and sacred task, and that if they succeed in bringing light and help, knowledge and health to those who before were lost in the mists, then indeed they are fulfilling the purpose of their beings.

We remember, too, all those in other worlds who for long

have been engaged in the task of inspiring instruments everywhere to greater service, so that they can bring children of the Great Spirit nearer to the power which fashioned them and thus help them to live the kind of radiant life which comes to all those who are crowned with truth and knowledge.

This is the prayer of Thy Indian Servant who seeks always to serve.

Chapter 4

'LOVE IS THE KEY'

ALL major religions teach the reality of life after death. Spiritualism stands alone in that mediums—those gifted channels of communication between this world and the next—are able to offer demonstrable evidence from those who have preceded us to the spirit world.

Yet, as all experienced Spiritualists know, results can never be guaranteed. Indeed it has to be admitted that some sittings fail. But why is this?

Silver Birch addressed himself to this problem on one occasion when there were no visitors to his circle. He took the opportunity to invite circle members to put questions to him, adding, "I do not want easy ones; I want hard nuts to crack."

One asked the guide to explain the failure of a recent sitting with a clairvoyant.

"Lack of development," was his reply, "a too speedy attempt to sit with strangers when the power has not had the opportunity of settling down to a stage where it can be easily moulded, and the subconsciousness of the instrument is not stilled sufficiently. All the time the impressions of the medium keep rising and they cannot be thrown away.

"The guide is there but cannot take complete control. In all phases of control, where there is not mastery by the guide, these impressions must be registered, otherwise nothing at all can come through."

"Is there any mediumship which is free from the subconscious mind?" asked another sitter.

"No," was the categorical response.

"It is all tinged," the questioner commented.

"It must be so, because every form of communication depends on the use of a human instrument. Wherever you have the human instrument that communication must be tinged by the channel through which it operates, because being a human channel it cannot be devoid of its own nature."

The questioner, a former Methodist minister, then asked, "If the Great Spirit is perfect, why was not some better form of communication devised rather than one necessarily incomplete?"

"I invited difficult questions and I am glad that you responded so freely," was the guide's comment. "You must realise that all the words we use are subject to definition. The Great Spirit is perfect, but not in all the expressions of its manifestation at the same time. Of itself the Great Spirit is perfection; in embryo, that portion of the Great Spirit which is within you is perfect, but not in its manifestation through physical form. That is why you have the processes of evolution going on ceaselessly throughout all centuries, for evolution consists in the refining, in the purging away of the dross to allow the gold to become exhibited, in cleaning imperfections away from the innate perfection.

"In any stage of evolution you can have only that communication which is commensurate with the stage that you have reached. If you had something which was too much in excess of your evolution, it would be so much out of your reach that it would mean nothing to you."

"When we are more evolved might we get some mechanical form of communication?" the guide was asked.

"You know my view on the subject," he answered. "I do not see the mechanical processes becoming perfected without the use of a human instrument. You must appreciate, first of all, the reason for communication, and primarily, it is love. Love governs all communication, whether it be the love founded on the relationship between people who knew one another on earth, or the love of service and the desire to help mankind that attracts unknowns to one another.

"Love is the key. It is more important to have communication, however faulty, than to have no communication, because it enables love to find itself. In all the attempts at mechanical communication you eliminate the factor of love. You are attempting, instead of the warm, vibrant, loving communication, to have what is equivalent to your telephone."

"Cannot you get warmth and love through a telephone?" the sitter persisted.

"Through it, but not of it," said Silver Birch.

"Is not that which comes through the important thing?" the guide was asked.

"Not in this case," he answered. "What is important is the result on the 'telephone,' which is the human instrument, and those who receive the communication. It is intended to stimulate the spiritual nature of all who are involved."

"Including the medium?" asked the sitter.

"Yes, because ultimately, you will have people in your world whose spirit is so developed that they will be able to achieve communication with our world naturally, spirit responding to spirit. Trying to thwart that by the introduction of a machine is not helping the plan of spiritual evolution. It is through man's spirit that evolution will come; it is through raising the spirit so that the divine comes to the top."

"So if we want the best evidence we will have to develop highly evolved mediums," commented the sitter.

"I was not thinking so much in the terms of evidence," said the guide, "but in terms of human development, remembering that the plan of life always is a cycle in which, at one stage, the Great Spirit is implanted so as to find fuller expression, and that fuller expression is constantly being developed and extended in processes of time. Do I make myself clear?"

"Yes, we understand," he was assured.

"To obtain the best results there must be an attraction between two worlds and the hightest attracting force is the power of love. Love calling to love is the reason why all the barriers between the two worlds get broken down."

"That is why mediumship suffers when it gets too much on a monetary basis."

"Yes, because implanted in the breast of the medium must be an overwhelming desire to serve, which, by virtue of its desire, raises the stature of the instrument. That is the most important of all, for without increasing spiritual development of the human race, the alternative is a very dreadful one. Strive to realise that the whole purpose of spirit return is to stimulate the divine in man, to help man to unfold the gifts of the spirit that he possesses in latent form, so that he may fulfil the purpose of his being."

"If somebody returns, say a father to his son, is that what he has in mind, or does he want to talk to his son?" Silver Birch was asked.

"The father desires to return to his son. But why does he desire? His desire is based on love. He loves his son; his son loves him. That love is the incentive for the father to break through all the barriers, to overcome all the obstacles. Having demonstrated the power of his love, triumphing over all difficulties, and shown his son that love lives on beyond what is called death, the effect of that should be to stimulate the spirit of the son which, through suffering caused by bereavement, should have found itself. And thus, what starts with a demonstration intended to be of comfort should end with the beginning of spiritual development. Does that answer you?"

"Yes, it does. In other words, the Great Spirit uses all these experiences in His plan of development."

"The whole purpose of life, here and hereafter, is the

development of the spiritual nature. That is why you incarnate into matter. If you live your life aright, you will so develop the spirit that it is ready, and death will come just at that moment when the spirit is ripe for the next stage of its existence. That is the plan of life. In our world the processes continue with the spiritual nature unfolding, each time casting away another sheath, so that the body becomes purer and purer, approximating, more and more, to the latent perfection which is manifesting itself."

"You can often see that in the physical body where certain people who live a bad life have evidence in their body of that life."

"It must be so," said Silver Birch. "As a man thinketh in his heart, so he must be. What a man does must reflect itself in his being. It is true in all planes of life, for is not the body the servant of the mind? Was not the body created by mind in the first place?"

Another sitter asked, "In the eyes of the spirit world, if a person sins in thought, is it as bad as sinning in deed?"

"The question can be answered in several ways. When you say sin, in the eyes of the spirit world, you mean, of course, from the standpoint of an evolved spiritual being?"

"Yes," he was told. Another member of the circle asked, "If you think a certain thing, has it the same bad effect as if you do it?"

"These are difficult questions," said the guide, "because unless one had a particular case cited it is hard to answer in a general strain."

"Supposing you wanted somebody killed?" he was told.

"It depends on the motive," was the guide's answer. "The first thing to do always in considering any problem is to say, 'What effect does it have on the spirit?' Thus, you say to yourself, 'What is the motive or the desire of the person who has the thought?' Now, that depends on the temperament of the individual. There are some who are willing to wound but afraid to strike. They are not prepared to go the whole way;

they are cowardly. They would like to hurt as much as they can without being too actively concerned in the performance of the deed itself.

"Is it as bad to think of killing an individual as to kill an individual? No! Because there is no power of thought which will have the effect, so far as your western world is concerned, of forcing that individual spirit out of the body, which the violent act of killing will do. Thus, in such a case, the thought, from a spiritual standpoint is not as bad as the deed.

"On the mental plane, jealousy, greed, envy, hatred, these can do more harm to the spirit of the person who allows himself to be influenced by them than many physical actions that he would perform, because the intensity of the thought power sent into operation might be more injurious to the spirit and mind of the person to whom they are attracted, than if the thinker were to strike a person a heavy blow. It is, of necessity, a question which requires qualification."

The answer produced this comment from a sitter: "You said that if a person wished somebody dead, it would not be so bad because by thinking they could not actually kill. Could it not be more harmful to the person who had the thought?"

"Yes," said the guide. "Again these questions and answers are subject to qualification, because it depends on the degree of the intensity of the desire. Try to realise that what controls it is cause and effect, the natural law in operation which is immutable and is so designed on the mental and spiritual planes to bring results as a physical action in your world brings results. What you cannot see is the effect on the mind or the spirit of the person who thinks these things."

"Is it ever right to hate anybody or anything?" the same questioner asked. "Do you ever hate anybody or anything?"

"It is easy for me to answer the last part of the question first. I do not hate anybody; I cannot hate anybody, because I see in every child of the Great Spirit a portion of divinity, and I am always filled with compassion when I find that the expression is either practically non-existent or very small.

But I can hate systems and desire that they shall be abolished. I can become angry when I see cruelty, when I see the results of greed and malice and the lust for power. Then I can be filled with thoughts that are far from kind, but you must remember I am very human. I have evolved sufficiently not to feel like that towards any human being."

"Even although they are responsible?"

"Yes, my son," was the guide's answer.

"Even I can understand that," said another circle member. "It is a terrible thing to hate."

"I know wicked men who have been responsible for misery and I am afraid I do hate them," declared the first member.

"I cannot," asserted the guide, "because I know the law, I know that the Great Spirit is not mocked, and whatever any man does he will pay the price in your world or in mine. None escapes the consequences of any action, word or thought. And so I cannot find it in myself to hate those who wear, however shabbily, the divine garment that has been given to them. But I can hate iniquity."

"In business today there are some very wicked men," persisted the first questioner.

"Then, feel sorry for them," said the guide.

"I don't think I can be very evolved, I feel hate," confessed the member, while another declared, "I have not come across that, but I do feel passion at the ill-treating of animals."

Silver Birch's comment was, "You must remember that these people are victims of their own lack of evolution, blind creatures who have lost their way. It is very sad."

Still the original questioner persisted with: "A lot of them are men of intelligence and brain. They exploit people who have not their gifts and I hate it."

"They are punished, they punish themselves," was the spirit rejoinder. "The difference between us is that you view your world through eyes of matter and I see it through the eyes of spirit. I know the suffering they will bring on themselves for centuries that lie in front of them. The soul will writhe in the agony of darkness, lost in the mists where remorse will bring its own punishment."

"In the meantime they bring so much suffering to other people's lives."

"How else would you have it?" asked the guide. "Would you have free will withdrawn and man reduced to a puppet? If you give the blessed opportunity of free will being exercised so that it can rise to the heights of superb divinity, you must allow for that free will to take the wrong turning and to descend to the utter depths."

Another member asked, "What is the effect on the mind of the man who has the bad thought—not the result of the thought?"

"If it is done cold-bloodedly, as distinct from inflamed passion, I would still abide by my answer because that would indicate the stage of development, or lack of development, reached by the individual. If he had attained the stage that, not only does he think of killing, he is prepared to translate it into action, then I would say that he has sinned far more than if he stopped short at the thought."

"He might stop because he is a coward,"

"I exempted the coward. I was taking the case of the person who cold-bloodedly goes through with the whole thing. I said this is the kind of question that would require many definitions. If it resolves itself into two individuals, one who not only thinks seriously and constantly of killing, and then decides to translate the thought into deed, and the other who says, 'I wish I could kill someone because I dislike or hate him so much,' then I would say the first is the worst so far as spiritual law is concerned."

Then Silver Birch was asked, "What is your own personal, most important, unanswered question?"

"I do not know if I have any important ones that are unanswered, except that I find it sometimes very hard to understand why the plan should have been formulated to achieve a perfection that in the very nature of the plan could not be achieved. It is a point on which I have spent much time and consultation, but I must say I am never satisfied with the answers I have got."

"Isn't it that the Great Spirit is not perfect Himself?" said a sitter, who added, "but you always say He is."

"We are getting into deeper waters, much deeper than we have ventured hitherto," said the guide. "I am forced to use the terminology of the earthly word, and so we get to a Great Spirit that becomes a He, a male, and that is not the Great Spirit that I know. The Great Spirit that I know is the infinite intelligence between the perfect, natural laws. That intelligence is displayed in a multitude of manifestations. I would not claim that I have seen the highest, for as far as I have reached I realise that there are summits beyond.

"I know, in outline, the plan of the universe as I have seen it. I cannot claim to fill in every detail—I have said to you that you, like I, must let faith take you in those regions where knowledge cannot go. Perfection, like the Great Spirit, is something that cannot be completely understood while you yourselves are imperfect. As far as I have gone, I fail to understand why it should be part of the plan for mankind to achieve perfection which in the very nature of the plan it cannot achieve, because its achievement would mean a cessation, and a cessation would be a contradiction of evolution."

"Just as we come to you with our problems, have you some higher court you can reach?" Silver Birch was asked.

"When I report to the inner spheres, there are individuals who are far wiser than I."

"Do you have the same sort of sitting?"

"We have our counsellors and our teachers."

"Do they go into trance?"

"The process is not quite analogous, but it does consist of a bringing down of vibration, of transmuting the higher to the lower to reach us, a shading of some light to enable the individuals to be at home on our level. That is akin to mediumship. If you get into your minds this picture of graded life in the universe and know that, no matter what rung of the ladder you reach, there is one above it and that this ladder of Jacob is infinite in its rungs—none can see the highest or the lowest."

The next question was: "Are our spirit friends really as close to us as they seem to be, or must we take into consideration the subconscious mind of the medium? Is it really quite as easy as it sounds? My feeling is that they do not get quite so close as we think they do. It seems too easy."

"What is too easy?" asked Silver Birch.

"I do not see how you can get so close as you seem to do. The more you have sittings with mediums, the more you realise it is not the spirit to whom you are supposed to be talking. Sometimes I feel that you are not talking to them at all—they have just put an impression through."

"As to our reality, let there be no doubt," answered the guide. "As to our individuality, there can be no doubt. As to who we are, there are differences of opinion, because of different approaches to the understanding of what is meant by identity. I am not concerned with the physical name that was chosen for you by your parents. To me, there is a difference between the name and the individual who bears the name.

"When it comes to what we are, the answer is dependent on what you mean by identity. I am not an Indian, as you know, although I constantly use the form of an Indian, because I find it is the easiest way of expressing myself through this instrument. The reality of guides cannot be disputed, but the question of the impact of spirit on matter is full of complications and is subject to a variety of happenings which can affect communication and alter its character.

"The degrees that can be manifested are varying in quality and quantity dependent on a host of factors operating at the time. The question of guidance is one that bristles with difficulty because you think of guidance in terms of what you want at a particular time, but that need not be guidance at all. It often is true that the best guidance for you to receive is not that for which you ask and, indeed, the refusal to give you that for which you ask is the best for your soul.

"It is not an easy question to deal with summarily because in the problem of guidance is bound up the whole problem of the consciousness, the progress and the awareness of the individual who is concerned. You realise you are not touching on simple matters. I have heard prayers from your world many times. I get requests, but I stand aside sometimes when I would like to help. I have sometimes rushed to help and a superior power has said, 'Hold on!' I cannot always exercise my free will, having promised to work within the prescribed law.

"I am not going to say that it is always easy, or that it is always difficult. Sometimes it is easy, sometimes it is difficult. But remember that often your shadow is our light and your light is our shadow. Your sunshine is our storm and your quietness is our noise, and your noise is our quietness.

"Your reality is not ours. We are not living in the same world even though we exist in the same universe. The whole of your philosophy and outlook are conditioned and controlled by your purely physical approach. You cannot see with the eyes of the spirit and often, unwittingly, you condemn or criticise, and, I do not speak harshly, because your vision is short. You cannot see all the way.

"That we are far from perfect, I am the first to admit. That we cannot do all we would like, I would not deny. But that is far different from the realisation that we are as close to you as the beating of your own heart, that we are closer than the shadow you cause when you walk in the path of the sun, that all you who come within the orbit of my love are as close as one spirit can be to another. I cannot always demonstrate that closeness in physical measurement. I could demonstrate it in spiritual understanding, but alas, and again I say this is no criticism, the times when your spirits can rise to that height are unfortunately too few. I do not blame you. That is the measure of the progress you have yet to obtain.

"Your criticism may seem just, but it is short-sighted and does not cover all the facts. Nevertheless our shoulders must be broad, for the teacher must be willing to take all that comes from the pupil, realising that the mere act of expressing these thoughts is an indication that the soul is marching on the road to progress. Do not fear that I will resent an honest question. I welcome it. Anything that you would say or do, any of you, could not diminish, by one iota, the great, tender love that I have for all of you."

"We have it for you. These are purely questions of a searching mind."

"I do not say any of this in any spirit of criticism. We are all divine and human, full of complexities, simple yet profound. As the soul unfolds, it moves to simplicity, but also nearer to profundity. These are opposite ends of the same pole. There is a scientific law that action and reaction are both opposite and equal. It is not easy, neither was it intended that it should be easy. We are fellow-pilgrims on the road of life and the staff of knowledge that we carry will help our feet when the going is hard. Hold on to the staff; it is your knowledge. Without it you cannot travel the road."

"I suppose we are too close to our own development to see it," commented a sitter.

"I always tell you two things which are important. One is when you enter the realm where knowledge cannot help you, then rely on that faith which in the first place was founded on knowledge. The other is, use your reason. It is the Great Spirit's gift to you. Never fail to reject that which does not measure up to the standard of your reasonableness, for your reason will develop and grow, and thus your standards will increase. Like all statements which seem contradictory it is but a paradox and paradoxes are the emblems of truth.

"When your reason asks questions I do not condemn it; I rejoice because the fact that it is asking questions means that the soul is stirring and that always gives me cause for rejoicing.

"I hope I have acquitted myself fairly well," said the guide. And then, with a smile he said to the former Methodist minister, "When the examination paper comes round, mark mine with charity and kindness."

'Now we strive through many'

"Oh Great White Spirit, Thou art beyond all definition and explanation because Thou art infinite. No book, no church, no building and no language can contain the whole of Thee, nor explain fully what Thou art.

"In days gone by, a privileged few received inspiration from the world unseen and it enabled them to get clearer glimpses of the supernal world and the denizens who dwell in it. But all their inspiration was limited to their mental and spiritual evolution and their conceptions of Thee were distorted, imperfect and incomplete.

"Now we strive through many, and not the few, to reveal a truer concept of the infinite mind that is behind the whole of the universe. We teach of the natural law which reigns supreme, which knows of no exception, no alteration and of no abrogation.

"We teach that the natural law is responsible for the whole of life, even for that part which is not manifested in a world of matter. We teach that the natural law controls every facet of activity and all come within its scope.

"Thus the law, which an infinite mind has conceived, and operates through love and wisdom, takes cognisance of every aspect of universal life. All who dwell on earth come within its ken.

"Thy spirit which has shaped all life is also within every one of Thy earthly children. The divine tie is eternal. That which binds them to Thee will last beyond the grave and in the worlds beyond that.

"If Thy children understood Thee they would understand themselves and they would look within their own beings to find mirrored there the pattern of Thy perfection; dormant, latent, ineffable, it still is there, waiting to be called up into greater expression.

"As Thy children learn more about the laws of life, they can order their own activities so that greater expression will be given to the divine spirit which is within them. Thus will they find peace and tranquillity; thus will they find the source of strength and confidence; thus will they learn to tap the reservoir of the spirit and draw from it all that is necessary to equip them for their daily lives and to help them in the hours of difficulty and of trial.

"And by calling upon the selfsame gifts of the spirit they will learn to enjoy fuller and richer communion with the liberated beings in a higher world who will be able to pour out on them the fruits of their knowledge, learning and wisdom and help to make the earth a fairer, richer and more beauteous place.

"By so doing there will be abolished much of the needless tragedy, the sorrow and anxiety, for knowledge will reign where ignorance is now prevalent. Health will drive out disease, comfort will replace sorrow and the light of truth reign where darkness has for too long held sway.

"To this end we labour with a great company who are dedicated to the purpose of serving Thy children everywhere. This is the prayer of Thy Indian servant who seeks to serve."

Chapter 5

'THERE IS NO JUDGEMENT'

SPRING always received special mention from Silver Birch. In all the years that he manifested, the spirit sage never failed to draw attention to the healing properties that accompany nature's own resurrection story. Here are the words he used at one sitting:

"This is the time of the year which makes my heart rejoice and makes me want to utter pæans of praise, for it is now that your world takes on great beauty, although the fullness will not yet be reached. It is in the awakening, in the abundant signs of rising, growing, unfolding life that we see evidence that the Great Spirit rules the universe. On every hand, flower, leaf and bush pay tribute to the constancy of natural law; can we not the more easily see and recognise that the Great Spirit has equally made provision for each one of us and that in our own lives these laws will not fail us?

"This is the reason why Spring should enable you to sound a note of optimism and confidence and to be completely satisfied that the fact of your birth is proof that your life is directed by love and wisdom which seek to use you in the service of those who require your help. Let your hearts and spirits rejoice in what is not a miracle, although it seems so, but an expression of the natural law which has not failed throughout all the centuries and will not fail through centuries which are yet to unfold their tale among the denizens of earth."

The guide was asked about the health of one of his earthly friends and replied: "You cannot ignore the requirements of nature. You are in a physical world, although you are spiritual beings, but your spirit can express itself only through the vehicle which you provide and that vehicle, being made of matter, has to conform to certain material requirements. It must have exercise, food, growth, shelter, light, air and a certain amount of attention. If it gets tired it must be rested; if some organs or functions become impaired they must be rectified. You cannot be indifferent to the physical requirements of your body without paying the price.

"You can take all the medicines from the doctors, but these can never be substitutes for that which the Great Spirit has provided. They will alleviate, they will act as palliatives, but they cannot really cure. They can deaden and soften and stimulate where necessary, but your body wants that which nature will freely give it. That is why I always urge upon you that when Springtime comes you must take advantage of it.

"All the new life, which is to express itself, brings with it the greatest recuperative forces. It must be so. And if you will add that to your own store you will recharge your batteries. Your vitality, which perforce must become lower during the time of winter, will be increased. If you are wise, and add generously to the stock, then you should have a sufficient store to maintain you through the autumn and winter when life, so far as the physical phenomena of nature are concerned, goes to sleep and into retirement. So fill your beings with what the Great Spirit freely and lavishly desires to bestow on you."

"Why is it that so many brilliant men simply cannot understand it?" inquired a sitter.

"You can have brilliance of brain without an understanding mind. 'Except ye become as little children.' Many great truths are simple and are thus instinctively perceived by those who are simple in heart and who require no complicated system to follow. There is a danger that where you have brilliance of brain there is a tendency to move away from simple truth because it no longer appeals. The brain does not get enough exercise when a fact is too simple. If it is complicated then the brain gets exercise and if it is a brilliant one it thinks this is what it requires. What must be obvious is that the more healthy your body the more it is in accord with the requirements of natural law."

"And the better your brain functions," put in the questioner.

"Yes, and the more easily the spirit expresses itself, otherwise you force upon it endless difficulties. A healthy body is easier for the mind and the spirit to manifest through than an unhealthy one, because, after all, it is only through the body that spirit can be made manifest on earth. You look at the animal kingdom and see how automatically when the sun shines the cats begin to lie in its healing warm rays, moving their position as the sun changes. They understand the simple truth which is instinctive to their beings.

"Man, unfortunately, through processes of civilisation, becomes more and more artificial. Too much smoking, drinking, stimulants—all these are wrong. The body does not really require them if it is living according to the dictates of natural law. If it is not, then of course it must have these stimulants, otherwise you have no appetites."

The subject was changed as one member asked, "Are you really satisfied with the way things are going these days as far as our movement is concerned?"

"I am never satisfied. I am happy wherever I see truth spreading. But your organised movement is passing through a difficult and unattractive phase. The original incentives, which first attracted by their brilliant lustre, have become tarnished and there is not enough direction. The greatest efforts should always be made, in my judgement, in giving truth to those who have it not, and to those who have it, they should be taught how to increase their capacity to receive more truth. Going out into the highways and byways still is the necessary task.

"Take the vital factor of mediumship, which is the whole basis and foundation for the movement of what is called Spiritualism. Is it to be seen at its best? Is the spirit of service a paramount idea among the majority of those who possess psychic gifts? Do they realise that theirs indeed is a sacred office and that they should approach it with reverence? There are some who do, there are, alas, many who do not.

"It is only among the older ones, speaking generally, that the desire for service exists in the form which I like best. Too many, alas, are less concerned with utilising their gifts to comfort mourners and to help the needy. They are too often interested in themselves. That is a phase which I hope will pass."

Later a member expressed the view that there were many things she did not understand about Spiritualism. "I find it so perplexing," she said.

"It is not possible in one incarnation on earth to have all the knowledge," answered Silver Birch.

"But the fact that we have some and do so little, I find it absolutely perplexing," she said.

"Knowledge, that is the unshakable foundation, and where you meet with perplexity and cannot find the answer, hold on to the knowledge which proves that the Great Spirit does rule wisely and well, and what seems difficult now will be made clear. That is not an evasion."

"I know," said the sitter. "We are responsible people and we are responsible for all we do. It is perplexing that we cannot progress through knowledge."

The guide answered: "There are laws within laws. There are laws that control the individual as well as those that control the growth of life, as well as those which are responsible for the evolution of the country and the race. All these work within one another. Unless you have the key, which is infinite wisdom, you cannot always see that there is perfect harmony throughout the whole framework. But there is."

"What I find very difficult to understand," continued the sitter, "is the relationship of guides to the people that they guide and their friends. There does not seem to be the understanding and the co-operation that one fondly imagines. The time comes when so many things are so hard to understand."

"There is a limitation to anything that the most evolved guide can do in your world. It is a limitation imposed by natural law, by circumstance and by free will. There is also a combination of factors which determines the precise amount of guidance that can be available at any moment. But what you do not know, and I cannot prove to you, is the unseen guidance that you get—how you are given ideas and inspiration and help in ways that are not revealed through mediums. These are intricate, difficult operations to perform and remember always that we are dependent on such fine and delicate vibrations for our results. And then you can have the exercise of free will which upsets it all."

"And surprise even you?"

"We cannot always know because our vision is not constant. It is in flashes, dependent upon certain processes where we can become *en rapport* with certain events. You can pick up a telescope, focus it accurately and see, but sometimes when all is prepared, one puff of cloud will come and you will see nothing. It is like that: you can get the focus right, the vision clear, and then a blur. There is a tiny movement and the whole focus is distorted. You can use, when you know how, the equivalent of an organ of sight in our world and by making all the adjustments, get glimpses, but this is a very difficult operation.

"What we can do is to follow a pattern, because we know the end to be attained, and within that pattern work with balance, tension, stress, adjustment all the time. It is like a game of chess. Sometimes if the wrong move is made we have to bring out the other pieces which counteract that. Sometimes we can influence all the right moves to be made for a little while. It is a very complicated matter. The regulation of spirit power in a material world where you are dealing with vibrations or radiations at two extreme rates causes a large number of adjustments constantly to be made. But the end is certain though the means are not always clear. That is why I often say, 'Wait, it is not the end of the story.'

"The laws work themselves out—they must do. And they cannot always follow the line that you would like. I know the task that I have to fulfil. I know the task that all of you have to fulfil in your earthly life. I am conscious that you will fulfil it. It is not an accident; it is part of a plan. You cannot understand the plan because you can see it only through physical eyes and measure it only with physical measurement. I, however, see it from a totally different aspect. While recognising all your material problems, and participating in them, I know fundamentally what is to be achieved.

"When the balance is struck, it will be found that the Great Spirit does not err. The intelligence behind the universe is perfect. Let there be no mistake about that. The Great Spirit does not err, neither can the Great Spirit be deceived. The laws will work inexorably in every case."

At another gathering of the circle, Silver Birch discussed the relationship between spirit and matter. The guests were a husband and wife keen on inquiring into Spiritualism. The guide told them:

"You are material beings; you are in a material world. You have certain obligations to discharge. Your body has to be clothed, housed, fed and cared for. It has to receive all that which is necessary for the work that it is called upon to do. The reason for your body's existence primarily is to be the vehicle of the spirit; apart from that your body has no existence. There are very few people in your world who know that. The body exists in the first place because of the spirit, and when the spirit withdraws the body collapses, disintegrates, dies.

"I say this to you because, like many people, you have not yet what I call the correct perspective. You do not view yourself as a spiritual being with a temporary earth life. You are inclined to allow the obligations of your body and your world to weigh more heavily upon you than they need do. Tell me if I am wrong; I do not mind being corrected."

"No, I think you are right," said the wife. "It is very difficult for us to realise and remember that."

"I know that. If you can change your perspective and realise that not only your bodies, but the world in which you live, and everything which it contains, all owe their existence to spirit, and that you are spirit and possess by virtue of being spirit all that the Great Spirit possesses, then you will understand that you have at your disposal a power which can enable you to triumph over every difficulty that comes your way. The source of life, the source of being, the source of eternity is within the spirit. If you can learn how to adjust yourself you can draw on that infinite reservoir to which I have referred.

"Spirit is not subjected to the limitations of matter. Spirit, which provides the dynamic of all life, the mainspring of all existence, will provide you with all that you require in your earthly life. The purpose of your being here is a very simple one. It is to fortify, to equip, to unfold that spiritual nature which is yours, so that you are prepared for the next stage beyond death. Thus, every experience, good or bad, sunshine and shadow, strength and weakness, love and hate, health and sickness, adds its quota to your spiritual growth.

"Each has its place in the divine scheme. None of the darker experiences—dark to you that is because you do not like them—is so strong that you cannot overcome it. You will not be called upon during your earth life to face any test or crisis which you do not possess the strength to overcome. If I can make every soul I reach not only know that but feel it and live it, then they would be in harmony with the Great Spirit, and the laws of the Great Spirit and would be supplying themselves with all that they require from day to day, from hour to hour, from minute to minute, if you like. But there are the great enemies, fear, worry, anxiety. These are the foes because they set up conditions which disturb and prevent the very help that you want to receive. Calmness, confidence, receptivity, with these the spirit can flourish; with these you will find all you want from day to day; they will provide all that is necessary for the physical well-being."

The husband asked, "I would like to know what attention one must pay to this vehicle of the spirit; where is the culminating point?"

"It is not very difficult to arrive at the answer. If you look at most people I think you will agree with me that they are concerned with the requirements of their physical bodies and unconcerned with the requirements of their minds or their spirits. If as many people who are concerned with the needs of their physical bodies were to transfer part of that concern to the needs of their spirits, then your world would soon become a much better place than it is."

"Is not that person neglecting his spirit?" asked the husband. "Does it mean that he must take less care of his body, or should he increase his efforts altogether?"

"It depends on the individual, but, generally speaking, people do not neglect their bodies, they over-indulge them; they provide the body with far more than it requires. The conditions of what you call civilisation impose a lot of unnecessary obligations, and to meet the demands of convention you incur fresh obligations. The essential things of the body are light, air, food, exercise, shelter. I hesitate about clothing, but conventionally there is a need.

"I never preach the gospel that the body and its requirements should be neglected. Is not the body the instrument of the spirit? I am not asking that the requirements of the physical nature should be overlooked. All I am trying to do is to give to as many as will listen the right perspective, so that they will see themselves as they truly are. There are too many who think of themselves either as bodies only, or as bodies with spirits, whereas they are spirits with bodies. It is a tremendous difference. I see too many people in your world needlessly concerned with fears. It is the needless anxiety that I would strive to banish, because the Great Spirit is infinite in wisdom and in love. The wisdom and love of the Great Spirit transcend all our comprehension of these qualities.

"We see the results of this handiwork in universal activity. This universe, wondrous in design, is controlled and regulated and sustained by natural laws which have never failed. No mistake has ever been made in the execution of these laws; they have never been changed; they have never been repealed or supplemented. The natural laws that are in existence now were always in existence and will always be in existence because they were designed by perfection, created by omnipotence. Look round the universe where you like and see that every aspect, whether it be majestically large or microscopically small, lives, moves, behaves, and is regulated by natural law.

"Whether you turn to the vast galaxies or examine the most minute speck of life; whether you turn to the ever-changing panorama of nature's handiwork, whether you fix your gaze on bird, tree, flower, sea, ocean, river, lake, all is regulated by law which has provided for every aspect, as the earth spins on its axis for the seasons' variety to follow one another. Does growth not follow that which has been sown? Is not always this unchanging standard the divine pattern? The Great Spirit has not failed. The Great Spirit will not fail you if you allow the Great Spirit not to fail you.

"That is the perspective which I desire all children of the Great Spirit to possess. Then they would have no fear and no trembling. They would know that each experience, whatever it was, could only help in the growth of their soul. They would face it with that knowledge and thus they would pass every test. This is true although you may not see it at the time. When you come to our world, as come you will, it is the dark experiences for which you will express gratitude. It is the storm and the shadow for which you will be thankful, for you will realise, in your changed viewpoint, that these experiences, so unwelcome at the time, were the means by which the spirit grew. I cannot prove that to you, but you will prove it for yourself one day.

"This truth is of comparative newness to you. It is a large truth and has many aspects. There is much to learn; go on seeking. Do not accept all that which comes to you through the lips of the instruments who are used. Discard that which makes your reason revolt, or insults your intelligence. Accept that which seems reasonable and worth while. You are not asked to be credulous. You are asked only to accept that which is in consonance with your own judgement.

"We use fallible instruments. Sometimes the conditions of communication are not good; mistakes are made, and the entirety of what we desire to say does not succeed in being transmitted. Sometimes there are other difficulties, the health conditions of the instrument, the thoughts that are in the subconscious mind, dominant thoughts, perhaps, interfering with the processes of transmission. Then above all, never forget that we ourselves are fallible beings. Death has not given us the acquisition of the entirety of infinite knowledge. We see a little farther along the road of truth. Because we have gained a little more knowledge than you have we desire to share it with you. There is much that we do not know, but we strive to learn.

"What we have discovered in this larger life which has helped us we offer you so that it may help you, in the hope that having been helped yourself you will help others less fortunate than you are. That is the whole scheme. It is very simple. For ourselves we desire nothing, no thanks, no adulation, no worship. We are but ministers, ambassadors of the Great Spirit, unworthy perhaps to perform this task. But we have been called upon to do it, have agreed to do so and will strive to perform it to the best of our ability."

A twice-widowed woman came to the circle and in the course of the evening Silver Birch said to her: "There are certain experiences in your earthly world which compel you to face reality. There are certain events that compel you to find the Great Spirit and yourself, to look within and without, to seek the pattern of the universe, to find if it is a mystery or a plan, to ask, 'Why? why? why?' and to see if you can find the answers. In these times of great crises you cannot always find the answers, though you may find some of them. The mere fact that you ask the question is an indication that the soul is coming into its own.

"Your earthly world is the place where the soul comes to learn. It is the world where you make your mistakes and I hope profit from them. This is where you can put right the things which you did wrong, learn your lessons, try to do better, succeed where you have failed. At some stage you will realise that it is not the attainment which is so important as the moulding of the character in striving to reach the attainment. Such experiences enable the scales to fall from the physical eyes and for a true assessment to be made of values, and in such an assessment the things of matter are not greatly important, although obviously they have their place. If as a result of living in the shadows, the soul comes into its own, finds itself, strengthens the links in the chain that unite it to the Great Spirit, then it has been worth while. At some time yet to come, you will look back in retrospect and express gratitude for those experiences which seemed so difficult, but proved to be milestones on the road of spiritual understanding."

The visitor was told of the presence of a much-loved animal, an Irish setter: "Your beautiful dog comes. The one who loved you as much as you loved him. I wish you could see him. No sign of age or infirmity, but beautiful in grace, in outline, a lovely gentle, affectionate creature whom you helped in his evolution. You are richly blessed. You have love from a human, and you have love from—I cannot call a dog an unhuman—from this beautiful creature. You are surrounded by love from other creatures in your earthly life. Where others do not feel and respond to the affection, you do."

Silver Birch said there was present one whom he called "the great saint"—Francis of Assisi.

"Does that surprise you?" he asked. "This man has love for all. He strives to serve the cause of the dumb animals whom the Great Spirit sent into the world to be the companions of man in his evolution, but who are too often ill-treated and made beasts of burden and misused and outraged for so-called knowledge that is of no value to the human race."

Later, the guide reverted to the theme of the needless fear he found in the minds of many people. One sitter said: "I do not live the life that you preach and therefore I have fears. If we do not do our job we cannot expect you to do yours and so one has fears. It is all wrong, I know."

"You think you are much worse than you are," said Silver Birch.

"No, I have not got any illusions. I do know when I am wrong and therefore I know if you do not live the right life you cannot go through life without fear."

"Permit me to disagree with you, not for the first time, and say that you are not so bad as you think you are, but not so good as you could be. But always those who have seen the light are more conscious of the darkness."

"We have to pay for it," said this sitter.

"You will have to pay; all will have to pay as the law does not permit any escapes."

"I am hoping we will be judged differently in the next world."

"There is no judgement. The soul comes into its own—cause and effect—you reap what you have sown; you are the result of what you have done, that is all. You cannot be better, you cannot be worse, you cannot be higher, you cannot be lower. You are what you are because of what you have done. That is all there is to it."

'Nothing happens by chance'

OH Great White Spirit, we approach the fountain-head of all life seeking to establish a closer union with that power which has fashioned us all in its own divine image and which holds the whole of humanity in its embrace of love.

We recognise that Thou art the Great Spirit and because Thou art infinite, we cannot comprehend the whole of Thy majesty. Neither can we understand the fullness of Thy supremacy. But we do recognise that throughout the whole of the universe, in all its multitudinous and infinite manifestations, Thy natural law reigns supreme and that the whole of both visible and what is called invisible is regulated by natural law which is unchanging, inflexible and inexorable.

Nothing happens by chance or by accident. All is due to the divine design which has made provision and which regulates every facet of activity. Nothing happens which is outside Thy knowledge or Thy care. No being is removed from Thee or forgotten by Thee. All come within the scope of Thy beneficent plan.

We pay tribute to the constancy and marvel of this law which overlooks none and throughout all time continues ceaselessly to work according to the pattern which infinite intelligence has devised and infinite wisdom sustains.

It is part of our task to make more understandable the operation of this law to those who are prepared to receive this knowledge, so that the scales may fall from their eyes, their ears and hearts become open and their souls flooded with the illumination of that great truth which will teach them the purpose of their being and make them realise the part they have to play in their own lives.

By doing so we will help to abolish darkness, ignorance, selfishness, evil, chaos, bankruptcy, bloodshed and misery which are foul excrescences in the world of matter and which owe their origin to the materialistic selfishness which is prevalent in so many places.

To this end we pray and labour. This is the prayer of Thy Indian servant who seeks always to serve.

Chapter 6

'KNOWLEDGE DISPELS FEAR'

A FEATURE of Silver Birch's philosophy was his constant emphasis on what he called "The Law." Man-made laws, of course, often alter with changed circumstances. Not so spiritual law. Silver Birch put it thus:

"The Great Spirit is infinite, and you are parts of the Great Spirit. If you have perfect faith and live your lives right, then you are able to participate in the bounty of the Great Spirit. If every person in your world had perfect faith, then he would receive. If a person were hungry and yet had perfect faith, then he would receive the answer.

"That is how the Law operates. If you learn to attune yourself to the Law, the results must come. If the results do not come, that only proves that you are not in tune with the Law. Your history books tell you that there have been those from the lowest of the low, the poorest of the poor, who have tried the Law and it has not failed them. You must not point to those who do not try it and ask why it does not work.

"Sometimes the spirit gets crushed and cannot rise above the surrounding circumstances, but if you have perfect faith you could rise above all the troubles of your world. You would turn your faces to the sun, which is but an emblem of the Great Spirit, and say: 'I am a part of the Great Spirit. I am indestructible. I am eternal. I am infinite. That which is finite and part of the world of matter cannot touch me.' If you did that, you would not be touched.

"Many people start with fear in their hearts. They are afraid they will not get results, and the element of fear disturbs the vibration. Perfect love casteth out fear. Seek ye first the kingdom of God and His righteousness, and all these things shall be added unto you.

"That was taught to you many years ago by one who knew the Law. He showed that when he put it into operation the results were always forthcoming. If you allow the Law to function, then the results must come.

"I will tell you another Law. There is nothing you can have in the world of matter without paying the price. The price of mediumship is increased sensitiveness. You cannot accumulate wealth without paying the price, because if you do that, and forget the duties of your own spirit, then you may be rich in the goods of your world, but you will be very poor in my world.

"You have the greatest riches within yourselves. You are part of the Great Spirit. There are no riches or fortunes in your world that can be compared with that. We seek to teach you to explore your own gold mines, to reveal the diamonds of the spirit that are within the clay of your own natures.

"May you all learn to respond to vibrations of the highest planes of spirit. May you all realise that you are never alone, but always encompassed around and about by a host of those who love you, who seek to guard and guide you and to help and inspire you. And may you, as you unfold your own spirits, realise that you are being drawn closer to the greatest Spirit of all, becoming more in unison with His Law.

"You serve Him by serving the children of matter. When you do that, you are within reach of His infinite arms, you are surrounded by His love, which will bring you to perfect peace.

"Faith, that is faith alone, sometimes fails when the winds of bitter experience blow. But the faith that is born of knowledge provides a foundation which is so strong that no wind of circumstance can disturb it.

"Blessed are those who believe and have not yet seen, but thrice blessed are they who know and, because they know, place their faith in that which is not yet revealed to them, because they know that the laws of the universe are operated by a power which is love and wisdom.

"You should all have perfect faith, because it is a faith born of knowledge. You have had the proof of the power of the spirit. Now you should have the faith that all things work wisely and well and that, if you put yourselves in tune with the laws of the Great Spirit, then you must reap the operation of those laws.

"You can all banish from your minds the thought that anything that is unenlightened—or, as you would say, evil—can ever touch you. You live and move under the protection of the Great Spirit and His laws.

"If there is no evil in your hearts, then only good can reach you, for only good can dwell where goodness reigns. None but the servants of the Great Spirit come into your presence from my world. You need have no fears. The power which envelops you, the power which supports and seeks to guide you and inspire you, is the power that emanates from the Great Spirit of all.

"That power can sustain you in all your trials and difficulties. That power can change your storms into sunshine, and bring you out of the darkness of despair into the light of knowledge. Your feet are set on pathways of progress. There is no need for fear.

"Perfect love casteth out fear. Knowledge dispels fear, for fear is born of ignorance. Where there is love and trust and knowledge, there fear cannot reign. An evolved spirit cannot be afraid at any time, because he knows there is no experience that can come to him in any phase of life that he cannot master, for he is the Great Spirit.

"Fear creates its own prison for the soul. You must learn to rise above fear and not to allow its vibrations to hinder you, to have perfect faith and confidence and trust, to know that you can stand on your feet and say: 'I am the Great Spirit and the wind of circumstance cannot shake me. I will rise triumphant over every difficulty because of the infinite power which is within my soul.' You have power over every circumstance. Would you limit the power of the infinite soul?

"The Great Spirit rules over that which is material and that which is spiritual. There are no divisions in His universal kingdom. Do not attempt to divide the life of matter from the life of spirit. They are not distinct and separate. They are parts of one indivisible life, for the things of matter react on the things of spirit and the things of spirit react on the things of matter.

"You have yet to learn that there are no difficulties which beset those blessed with the power of the spirit that they will not surmount, as long as they in return serve the Great White Spirit wherever they go.

"There are no obstacles in your world we cannot remove; it it is the law that they shall be removed. If, sometimes, the cross you have seems very hard to bear, remember that, although I would give up all my progress to take it away from you, it is better for you to carry it and to learn the lesson it brings. You must consider not only this life, but the whole of eternity.

"If you children of matter would remember that not only are you human but also divine, how much easier would it be for you to live your lives.

"Your troubles would melt away, your obstacles would be swept on one side. But you have little faith in the power that is within you. What you call human belongs to the world of matter. That which is divine belongs to the Great Spirit.

"Many years ago you were told to be in the world but not of the world. Because the people of your world have not the faith, then the law cannot be put into operation. You say one has more money and less worry than another. You do not know how their worries compare. The laws of the Great

Spirit cannot be cheated.

"You are on earth to build your character. It is the way you face your problems that makes your character. But there is no trouble in your world of matter which is greater than the power you have within you for overcoming it, because the troubles are of the earth, material, and you are part of the Great Spirit, divine.

"There is only one peace—the peace which comes to those who are at one with the Great Spirit, whose hearts beat as one with His great heart, whose wills are at one with His great will, who are at one in soul, mind and heart with the Great Spirit. Then there is peace, because they are in harmony with His laws. There is no other peace.

"I can only teach you the laws. You were told many years ago that the kingdom of heaven is within. It is not without. It is not to be found in the rush of the world of matter. It is to be found within the soul.

"So finely balanced and so perfect is the law that there can be no cheating. Not one person escapes his punishment, and not one loses his reward. Do not judge eternity with the eyes of matter. Do not judge the smaller when you have not seen the greater.

"Do not confuse the transient joys of earth with the enduring things of the spirit. They are tawdry and flimsy. You think in terms of the earth, while I see with the eyes of the spirit. I cannot alter the law to please you.

"If you ask all those who return to you from my side, you will find that they all say the law is perfect. They never want to return to the world of matter. You seek to find peace without. I try to show you the eternal peace within. The greatest riches are the riches of the spirit.

"Some people will always worry. Even in the world of spirit they will worry. They will worry because they will realise they could be more perfect, because they are not perfect instruments for the Great Spirit, because only through toil and stress will they outwork the imperfections of their natures and allow the divine to shine through.

"Do you think we are happy when we realise the work that has yet to be done? Do you think we do not worry when we see the children of matter denied that which is necessary for their sustenance, or when we hear the false teaching that is poured out in the name of the Great Spirit?

"Do you think we do not worry when we see darkness where there should be light, when men are imprisoned by desire when they could be free, when we see the chaos that has been caused in your world?

"We worry because our hearts are filled with pity, because we seek to enable the love of the Great Spirit to flow through us and you into your world of matter, where so many are denied the things that are their heritage. The Great Spirit has given them all things in abundance, but they are denied them. You cannot be a great soul when others starve and you are filled with plenty.

"The hardest part of our task is when we have to stand by, sometimes, and see you suffer. We know we must not help because it is a battle of your own spirit. If you win your battle, then we have won, too. If you lose, then we have lost. It is our battle all the time, but we must not lift a finger to help.

"Sometimes I have wept tears because I have seen suffering, and knew I must not help. That is the law. It has hurt me more than it has hurt the sufferer.

"If you do what you know is right, then you cannot do any more. If that means that sometimes you must deny yourself, then you must do it. One day a balance is struck.

"I cannot solve your problems for you. If I tell you what to do, that interferes with your free will. Once I start to tell my medium what he must do and what he must not do, that is the end of his free will. Then his progress begins to suffer.

"It is the way you settle your problems that develops what is within you. You do not develop the spirit when everything is easy and smooth, but when you have difficulties. But there are times when we feel justified in interfering with your judgement.

"I would interfere if a very vital principle were involved. If it meant that my work through my medium would be interrupted, then I would interfere so that the channel would still be free. But where the problems only affect my medium's own evolution, then they are his responsibility and he must work them out for himself."

Silver Birch once contributed to a discussion on gardening by members of his circle with these words:

"Sowing and reaping are part of the natural law which I wish was accepted by more people. It is in the cultivation of the fruits of the earth that you learn how inexorable are the laws of the Great Spirit. He who lives close to the soil and sees the operation of nature's law begins to appreciate the divine handiwork and to realise something of the Mind which has planned all in its orderly sequence.

"That which is garnered is that which has been sown. The seed is always true to its type. You cannot sow the seed of a potato and expect that a lettuce will grow. Always what has been sown will follow unswervingly the dictate of the natural law. And what is true in that realm of nature is equally true in the realm of human life and activity.

"He who lives selfishly must reap the results of selfishness. He who sins must reap the result of his sin. He who is intolerant, bigoted or selfish will reap the results of intolerance, bigotry and selfishness. The law is inexorable; the law is immutable. There is no religious exercise, there is no hymn, no prayer, no sacred book that can interpose and alter the sequence of cause and effect.

"The effect follows cause with methodical and mechanical certainty, and no one has the power, be he called priest or layman, to interfere with that natural process. He who desires the growth of the spirit must live that kind of life which alone can assure spiritual growth.

"The spirit grows through kindness, toleration, sympathy, love, service and doing of good works. Character evolves only when you allow the divine spirit to be made manifest in your daily lives. If you harbour unkind thoughts, thoughts of hatred, of malice, of vengeance, of selfishness, you yourself will be the victim and you yourself must pay the price in a warped, distorted and thwarted character.

"All law is a part of one vast law. All works in harmony because all is part of the divine plan. The lesson of it is that men and women throughout the whole world of matter must seek their salvation by working it out in their daily lives, and abandon all the false theology which teaches that it is possible to cast on to others the results and responsibilities of your own actions.

"Man is the gardener of his own soul. The Great Spirit has provided him with all that is necessary for it to grow in wisdom, grace and beauty. The implements are there, he has but to use them wisely and well."

On another occasion he declared: "The law is perfect in its operation. Effect always follows cause with mathematical precision. No individual has the power to alter by one hairbreadth the sequence of cause and effect. That which is reaped must be that which is sown, and the soul of every individual registers indelibly all the results of earthly life. He who has sinned against the law bears on his own soul the results of his earthly action, and there will be no progress until reparation has been made for every sinful deed."

To Silver Birch the law is God and God is the law: "There is no personal God apart from the one that human beings have created; there is no personal Devil apart from the one that human beings have created. There is no golden heaven, no fiery hell. These are the imaginings of those whose views are limited. The Great Spirit is the Law. Know that, and you have learned life's greatest secret, for once you realise the world is governed by unchangeable, unbreakable, immutable, omnipotent law, you know that justice is done and none can be forgotten in the great scheme of creation.

"That is why all is known. That is why nothing can be

omitted. That is why every facet of life finds its place in the universal scheme. That is why nothing can be overlooked, for the law embraces every aspect of life, no matter how tiny, no matter how large, for all is law. Nothing exists except the Law which makes its existence possible. The law reigns supreme. Man's free will creates confusion and obscures the working of the law in his mind, but the Law exists just the same and must operate. I know that theology has been a great curse to your world, but its day is practically done."

At a different circle gathering Silver Birch explained that spirit communication is no sporadic, unorganised affair. There is, he said, a plan behind it all. The guide added:

"Our work is to give that which has a purpose, a significance, so that, while it demonstrates the existence of law, it also enables comfort to be given and knowledge to be spread. Our work is not only to reveal the existence of laws beyond the physical but to reveal truths of the spirit.

"We have a gigantic system of misrepresentation to oppose. We have to undo the work of centuries. We have to destroy the superstructure of falsity that has been built upon the foundations of creeds.

"We are striving always to teach the children of matter how to be free and how to bask in the sunlight of spiritual truth, how to cast off the serfdom of creedal slavery. That is not an easy task, for once the trappings of religion have mastered you, it takes a long time for spiritual truth to penetrate that thick wall of superstition.

"We strive always to reveal the religious significance of spiritual truth, for when your world understands its spiritual import there will be a revolution mightier than all the revolutions of war and blood.

"It will be a revolution of the soul and, all over the world, people will claim what is their due—the right to enjoy to the full the liberties of the spirit. Away will go every restriction which has put fetters on them.

"Our allegiance is not to a Creed, not to a Book, not to a

Church, but to the Great Spirit of life and to His eternal natural laws.

"A great power of the spirit will descend into your world of matter. In all its countries a mighty force of the spirit will be felt, for there is a great work to be done to counteract the selfishness and ignorance of your world. In time it will conquer, but, in the process, there will be much travail.

"Plenty of workers have come to take their stand at your side. There are those who are known to you, those who are bound to you with ties of blood and others who are attracted to serve you out of the love that they bear for you. When you think of those whose names you know, try to realise the countless host of the unknown, who serve without any desire to be known or recognised but who give their power to be used.

"The world will not be converted in a blinding flash like Saul on the road to Damascus. Gradually, the light of spiritual truths will break through, as more people become aware of the great knowledge and more instruments are available for the power of the Great White Spirit to use. You must remember that the things of the spirit require careful nurture and progress. Sudden conversions would not be enduring, and our work is intended to be permanent.

"Each soul that becomes an instrument for the Great Spirit, each soul that moves out of darkness into the light, out of ignorance into knowledge, out of superstition into truth, is helping to advance the world, for each one of these is a nail that is driven into the coffin of the world's materialism.

"What you must all learn is that there are two forms of development. You can unfold that which is of the soul and you can unfold that which is of the spirit. One is the development of only the psychic faculty, and the other is soul-growth.

"Where you get the development of the psychic without the spiritual, there you have a low plane of vibration. When you get a combination of both, then you have not only a great medium but a great man or woman.

"What a glorious message we have for your world of matter—a message that makes men free and teaches them to rejoice in their divine heritage; a message that teaches them to throw off all shackles and bonds; a message that teaches them to rejoice in the fullness of spiritual knowledge; a message that shows them how to live not only on the planes of matter, but on the planes of spirit; a message that brings them beauty, love and wisdom, understanding, truth and happiness; a message that speaks of service, service, service.

"And yet we are denied by those who do not understand the revelation of the Great Spirit and who deny the spirit, as the power of the spirit has been denied throughout all times.

"The work that we do becomes more and more necessary. Your world is full of bloodshed, tears of misery and bitterness. In its blindness, your world will not live according to the laws of the Great Spirit. It has chosen the path that leads to darkness and to despair. We offer the knowledge that leads to hope, to light, to peace and to harmony. Your world may despise us, in its ignorance. It may reject the message that we bring. It may deny the power that accompanies us. But our great truth must prevail, for it is of the Great Spirit.

"Those who strive to live against the law reap for themselves the results of a bitter harvest. Those who live with the law reap a harvest of happiness and plenty, in the things of matter and in the things of the spirit.

"Through all the darkness that prevails, do not abandon hope, but be assured in the knowledge that those who work with you for the upliftment of humankind, who strive to bring better conditions into your world of matter, will prevail, for the power that is on their side is the mightiest power in the universe.

"You will not achieve that which is worth achieving without travail, without sorrow. Your world must learn its lessons in the only way it can learn them. We are breaking through all over the world of matter. Our message illumines minds in every part of your world, and, as the light of the spirit breaks in on your world, so its rays disperse the darkness of your materialism.

"We do not seek to terrify you with threats of punishment. We do not seek to make you craven cowards, living your lives because of fear. We strive to make you realise the latent divinity that is yours, that you may express more of the Great Spirit, that you may rise to greater heights and fill your mind with greater truth and wisdom.

"We urge you to be dissatisfied with what you have already received, because only through discontent and the desire to reach out can greater knowledge come. He who is satisfied stagnates: he who is discontented struggles towards greater freedom.

"We never say to you, 'Do not use your reason, have faith only.' We say, 'Use that which the Great Spirit has given you. Test us. Examine us. If aught that we say is debasing, cruel or immoral, then reject us.'

"If we seek always to teach you to live nobler lives, lives of greater self-sacrifice and of idealism, then surely that demonstrates that the hall-mark of the Great Spirit is stamped upon our teaching.

"If we raise up one soul, if we give comfort to one who mourns, if we give hope to one who is faint-hearted, if we give strength to one who is weary, then has it not been worth doing?

"Think of the many whom our message disturbs, whom it puzzles, who are perplexed, who, bound to a creed, cannot escape—yet they hear the voice of freedom calling to their imprisoned souls and their minds struggle to be free.

"They are the ones for whom the message is intended, those to whom it comes as an incentive to reach out to what before was unattainable. All truth is but a stepping stone.

"If you hear through the lips of the medium through whom I address you that which makes your reason revolt, that which contradicts the love of the Great Spirit, that which is foolish, that which is an insult to your intelligence, then know that my day is done and I have failed.

"Though I have spoken to you many, many times, I do not think I have ever said anything which is contrary to the highest aspirations of the soul. For our appeal is always to the highest that is within you.

"The world must learn to perform its own salvation. There is no ready-made plan. There is no prepared, cut-and-dried system. Your world has to learn that, behind what it regards as the manifestations of life, there is the eternal reality of the spirit, that the children of matter are not only worldly beings but spiritual beings expressing themselves through bodies of matter.

"The bodies of matter must be as perfect as they can be made through having all the necessities of life freely at their disposal, as the Great Spirit would have them. Then their spirits must be freed from all dogmatic and credal trammels, so that they do not give allegiance to things that have no real or spiritual value, so that they work only for that which is true, so that the warring and the quarrelling and the strife over creeds and dogmas, which have held your world in chains for thousands of years, can be abolished.

"We preach the gospel of the spiritual brotherhood of all peoples, with the Great White Spirit as the common Father. What stands in the way is the earthly conception, the churches built on error, the usurping of privilege, the pride and the power of tyrants, petty tyrants who hold the whip hand.

"As our teaching grows in your world, it will mean the end of all separateness between peoples. It will mean the end of national barriers. It will mean the end of race distinctions, class distinctions, colour distinctions and all the distinctions between churches and chapels, temples, mosques and synagogues, for gradually all will learn that they have a part of the Great Spirit's truth and that the part enshrined in the heart of every other religion in no way contradicts that portion which is precious to them.

"So, out of the apparent confusion, the divine pattern will take its shape and harmony and peace will come. I tell you these things, so that you can understand part of the great plan, the part that we who return from the world of spirit play in it, and the part that each one of you must play in it before your earthly course is run.

"What we preach fits in with all the noble and elevated ideas that have come to the vision of all the reformers, all the saints, all the seers and all the idealists who have striven in every age to render service. Because they were great souls, their spiritual eyes caught glimpses of the life that could be, and that vision of beauty sustained them in all their adversity and struggle. They realised the spirit plan that, one day, will be put into practice, and so they strove to raise up the children of matter, to serve.

"Though they were vilified, though they were opposed and ridiculed by those they came to help, their work lived on, even as the work that is being done today in countless small temples, such as this, will live on, though many of the people will be forgotten. The mighty power of the spirit has been launched once again in your world of matter, and the children of matter do not possess the power to stem that mighty tide.

"Your world thinks it solves its problems by the shedding of blood. But no problem was ever solved in that way, for bloodshed is needless and leads nowhere. Why cannot they use the reason which the Great Spirit has given them? Why do they think that their only solution must be to kill as many as possible, that the one who is the greatest killer is accounted the victor? It is a strange world you live in.

"Your world needs our message, the message of the spirit, the realisation of spirit truths, the knowledge that there are spiritual laws and guidance both from above and from within, so that in its perplexity it may learn where to turn to find comfort and guidance and help.

"We seek nothing for ourselves. We want no glory. We have simply the desire to be of service, to reveal once again the laws which have been forgotten, so that the world of matter may rediscover those powers of the spirit which can bring it new hope and new life.

"In your perplexity, when all the old standards are being discarded, when all authorities are being questioned and their power waning, we seek to reveal the Great Spirit, the supreme Authority, through His laws which never fail and which never err. If the world of matter will learn to order its life in accordance with those laws, peace and concord will rule once again.

"These things are part of the great mission which we all have to perform so that, amidst the crumbling ruins of the discarded beliefs, mankind may not reject all because of his doubt and scepticism, but may learn to sift the wheat from the chaff, the fact from the myth, and hold on to that which is precious, which is enshrined in all religions, the great truths of the spirit, long overlaid with the imaginations of the children of matter.

"The power of the spirit—which inspired those in days gone by, which gave them vision and courage, enthusiasm and desire to serve—is available today if the children of matter will learn to look for it in the operation of those laws which are at their disposal.

"The authority of Churches, of books, of creeds, all these are waning. They are gradually being discarded. But the authority of spiritual truths abides for ever. When I return to your world I see the confusion and the chaos, and I realise they could be dissipated if the clear light of the spirit were allowed to penetrate, if, instead of just a chink, there could be a strong illuminating ray.

"Why do they prefer the darkness when they could have the light? Why do they prefer ignorance when they could have knowledge? Why do they prefer superstition when they could have wisdom? Why do they prefer the dead bones of a creed when they could have the living truth of the spirit? Why do they prefer the dust of theology when they could have the waters of spiritual wisdom?

"There are souls blindly groping in self-imposed darkness, chained when they could be free, servile when they could easily be men of freedom. But I am afraid they have worn their chains for so long that they are afraid to discard them. A bird that is in a cage for a long time is afraid that it cannot fly when it is released.

"It is good when they throw off their shackles, but they must have some path which they can tread. We do not want them to be helpless, without a sign. We want them to be free, but we want them to know where their freedom will lead.

"When you have been in bondage for a long time, there is a tendency in the newly-found freedom that you will not listen to any guidance that comes to you. You say: 'I have had enough of all this. I have had years of doubt and perplexity. Now that I have discarded it I do not any longer wish to be associated with what is called religion.'

"Sometimes, with the casting off of shackles, there is a violent reaction. I do not want too much attention paid to me, the individual, the messenger. I am only concerned with the message. Your world has for too long concerned itself with teachers, whom it has aggrandised into exaggerated positions, and has forgotten what they came to teach.

"Our mission no longer is to exalt men and women into high places of authority, but to seek to reveal truth, knowledge and wisdom. What does it matter whether I am a teacher of great distinction or a lowly beggar, so long as the seal of truth stamps what I say? Our appeal is no longer to names and authorities and books, but to reason alone.

"We demand nothing that is contrary to your intelligence. We preach nothing that you can say is untrue, that is undignified, that is ignoble, that debases mankind. We seek to reveal that which will elevate the whole human race and give it a true conception of its position in life and in the universe, its relationship to the Great White Spirit and an understanding of its kinship with other members of the vast human family in your world.

"No longer will we resort to books or teachers or authorities, but only to divine reason, and we appeal to her. Our truth will not be spread by the citation of a text said to be stamped with divine authority. If it violates reason, then reject what we say. But you will find that we appeal to the highest and the best instincts, that we only seek to brush away old falsehood and to bring the great truth that man will prize. What your world calls religion must be founded on truth, and you must seek to discard all that will not stand the onslaught of reason.

"We strive to reveal these truths, not only as they are known in their relation to the laws of the spirit, but also to the laws of matter, for to us the world of matter is part of the universe of the Great Spirit, and you cannot be 'religious' if you are indifferent to the sufferings of despairing humanity. Those who serve are accounted as the great ones by us, and the service they render is not confined to helping the soul to find truth, for there is other service to be rendered.

"There is the service of freeing poor, racked bodies from pain, the service of fighting injustice and tyranny, the service of fighting hate, the service of preserving freedom and the service of abolishing the evils of your world and giving the spirit in man a chance to express itself as the Great Spirit desires that it should.

"I am sorry that the children of the Great Spirit have wandered so far from the things of the spirit that a rap on a table has to be used to make them understand His laws.

"You are all parts of the Great Spirit. He says to you: 'Here are all my laws and here, in you, is a part of me. Beside you there is all that can be used to make a perfect universe. I give you all the tools and you can choose between the things that are right and the things that are wrong. You can try to work with my laws or against them.'

"The children have chosen. But always those who are the masters in the world of spirit have to make sure that they incarnate into matter men who are so tuned to the vibrations of the Great Spirit that, through them, His work can go on. So far have the children wandered that they are blind to the things of the spirit and only understand things of matter.

"But after the storms and the wind have blown through the world there always comes the new life of the spring. When the snow lies on the ground and all looks very bleak, you are not able to see the freshness of the spring. But it comes.

"And gradually, as the great sun of life moves through the heavens of the Great Spirit, so the majesty of life comes to its fullest. Throughout the whole world of matter there is a great cloud of discontent. There will come the spring of dreams and the summer of fulfilment.

"It will come quickly or slowly as the children of the Great Spirit exercise their free will. But wherever in the world of matter one man strives to uplift one other man, then behind him there are a thousand spirits who try to make his victory a greater one. No effort for good can ever be lost. No desire to serve can ever be wasted.

"There must be a pioneer who hacks his way through the forest and makes the path a little easier for those who follow. Gradually the path is beaten down and worn smooth.

"Sometimes I see the many masters in my world, with tears in their eyes, looking down on the follies of those who, one day, will realise how they have thrown away the great opportunities they had of raising up the children of the earth. And sometimes I see their faces wreathed in smiles because, in your world, some unknown man has rendered a service which lights a new torch of hope in the world.

"I, like many others, have come nearer to the vibrations of the earth to help to push forward that great new world which waits just round the corner. I come to teach you the laws of the Great Spirit, and to show you how, if you live according to them, the bounty of the Great Spirit can be poured into your hearts and minds.

"I only see a world filled with sorrow that should be filled with happiness, darkness where there should be light, hunger where there should be plenty. I see that the Great Spirit has provided everything, and yet there are those who are preventing its distribution. There are obstacles which must be swept away.

"I cannot do it. I cannot even criticise. I can only tell you how the law can work if you, who are still encased in matter, will allow it to work through you. Those who do must point a finger of scorn to the things of earth and show the remedies of the Great Spirit.

"Show in your own lives you know the things of the spirit because the power of the spirit is in you. If, between us, we can in one case bring happiness where there was unhappiness, knowledge where there was ignorance, then at least we shall have done some service. We do not seek to take away from you the responsibilities of your own lives, but only to try to inspire you to live so that men may know the Great Spirit is working through you.

"It makes me sad, sometimes, to hear people say: 'Oh yes, we give them bread, but they must thank the Great Spirit first.' Why not give the bread and not worry whether they thank the Great Spirit or not? If a man is hungry, why not give him bread? Or they say: 'You can sleep here, but you must say a prayer.'

"Have you who possess this knowledge of Spiritualism ever tried to strike a balance? You have something that your world cannot measure. You have the priceless knowledge of the truths of the Great Spirit. You have the realisation that your soul is linked with His great soul. You have the knowledge that you are a part of the Great Spirit. You have learned how to respond to the vibrations of the messengers that the Great Spirit sends to watch over you.

"Compared with these things, the things of matter are as

mere baubles. You will live for many thousands of years. You will find that the knowledge you have gained here and the wisdom you have learned are of greater value to the life of your immortal soul than the few things that the body of matter seeks in the world of matter.

"Do not judge anything by the apparent result. You see only with the eyes of matter. If you could see with the eyes of the spirit, you would know that with every child there is perfect justice. Sometimes I listen to your prayers and sometimes to the prayers of others. I think that if the Great Spirit were to answer them all you would not be happy with the result.

"I have spoken to many who have crossed from your world to mine. I have not yet met one who has said when he saw with the eyes of the spirit, that he has not been served well by the Great Spirit.

"There are three great problems in the world of matter. One is ignorance, another is sorrow, and the third is poverty. These three things you will always have until knowledge of the spirit is joined with politics and the children of earth think and live as the new knowledge shows them.

"But the tide of victory rolls on. The old order dies giving place to the new. The new world is coming. But do not think that, because of this victory, there will be no more dark places. There will still be much shedding of tears. There will be many aching hearts. There is great sacrifice to be made.

"That which is a part of the Great Spirit cannot be achieved without sacrifice. You cannot build up unless you tear down. In times of great material disaster, the people of your world begin to examine the foundations of the things of the spirit. When all the things of matter have failed, they look for a reed to clutch, and they look into the systems that have been tried and found wanting.

"Then the truths of the spirit begin to emerge, and they begin to build their new world—a world where the laws of the Great Spirit begin to play their proper part. Until you do that, there will always be great troubles. The world will never become perfect, because the nearer perfection it becomes, the more will it realise the perfection in front of it."

'Man can reach out'

"OH Great White Spirit, we begin with Thee, for everything in this wondrous universe bears the hallmark of Thy infinity, for Thine is the intelligence which has devised it, Thine is the love which guides it and Thine is the wisdom which sustains it.

"Thy spirit broods over and through all its manifestations and Thy natural law takes cognisance of every aspect of its activity.

"It is Thy spirit which is seen in action in its highest in Thy children whom Thou has made like Thyself.

"Thou hast implanted within them the seed of Thine own divinity. Thus there is for all time the divine tie that cannot be severed throughout earthly life and all that lies beyond it.

"All who live, no matter where they may be, no matter what their station, their class, their colour, their race, their nationality, are part of Thy life, and Thy law sustains them all and Thy spirit is united with them all.

"Thus throughout all eternity they are bound to Thee. They cannot be lost or forgotten or neglected, for Thy unchanging, immutable law holds them in its embrace of love and wisdom.

"We desire to teach Thy children how to regulate their lives so that their spirits, minds and bodies may have a full manifestation, that man may be able to know his innate divinity and recognise his heritage and to claim that legacy which Thou has bequeathed to him in the shape of a full, rich and radiant life.

"With the exercise of the gifts of the spirit which Thou hast placed in human organisms, man can reach out beyond the confines of matter and have full communion with those larger souls who are freed from the thraldom of flesh and who return with love and with the desire to serve.

"In the union of the two states of being and in the abolition of all the handicaps that prevent the full flow of the power of the spirit, there will come to man such a fullness of inspiration that he will be able to enrich life with the lustre of the spirit, banish all the gloom and dissipate all the darkness in which for too long too many have lived.

"This is the prayer of Thy Indian servant who seeks to serve."

Chapter 7

'TO MASTER ETERNAL TRUTHS'

OVER the years literally hundreds upon hundreds of questions were put to the guide on just about any subject imaginable. And as this chapter proves Silver Birch always gave quite superb answers to the varied points put to him. Incidentally, the medium never knew in advance what points were to be raised.

What, for example, happens when we sleep? So asked a visitor, who had already read several books featuring the guide's teachings.

"In the sleep state there is a variety of experiences, ranging from the purely physical reaction to the spiritual activity," the guide began. "It is such a tremendous variety that you cannot point to any recollection and speak with certainty as to where in the range it fits.

"But the reason for sleep is simple. The body is a machine, a wondrous machine, more wonderful than the greatest engineers in your world could ever construct, and being a machine it has to rest, otherwise it could not maintain its efficiency.

"The other half of the story is that whilst the body, the machine, is resting, the spirit withdraws itself and is active. Truly you die every night, because the spirit is completely withdrawn from the body, with only the silver cord to maintain the link between the two. The spirit is freed from the body, apart from that tenuous link.

"During that state, the spirit freely roams in those aspects of our world, gravitating to those spheres which are natural to its growth and evolution. Unfortunately, the brain being the smaller, it cannot record the spirit experiences which are outside the realm of your time and sense dimensions.

"When you come to our world, when the cord is severed, you have complete recollection of every visit that you have made in your earthly sleep state. Now if you recollect, it is fragmentary; then it becomes permanent."

How do you call one another in the spirit world?

We are given names, when we get beyond the pull of earth, according to our attainments, so that the name is an expression of our spiritual growth and evolution. These do not matter. We recognise one another for what we are.

Is it true that persons can reincarnate into different races, thereby losing trace of their loved ones? This would appear to be a great calamity.

It does not present a proper picture of what is involved in reincarnation. It is not a calamity, because all human earthly relationships do not necessarily endure. When the Nazarene was in your world and they told him about his mother being present, he asked: "Who is my mother? Who is my father?"

The larger soul never incarnates in its entirety in matter. That portion of which you are aware in an earthly body is only a splinter and not the whole. Other splinters may incarnate at different periods and in different nationalities. The splinters may have earthly and even astral relationships, but these need not be a spiritual relationship.

What will always endure is the love, not the blood tie. If there are love and the blood tie, then the bond, because it is a willing bond, will continue. If there is a blood tie and there is no love, then the separation has taken place spiritually on earth and will continue in the worlds beyond yours.

Do people have the same guides and helpers throughout their life, or as they develop spiritually do the guides change?

It is dependent upon the work that has to be done. The guiding spirit, and we always work with groups or bands, is the one selected as the spokesman. If the task involved is to develop a particular form of mediumship that guiding spirit will prevail throughout the whole of the earth life. If the development is only a phase and there are other phases to be embraced, then other members of the group will advance to the fore.

You talk of the Great Spirit as "the law," and yet when you pray you use the term "Thee," implying a personality. To a lot of people this is rather conflicting.

This is the difficulty of language, to attempt to express in finite words that which is infinite and thus beyond language. Spirit, being superior to matter, cannot be contained in matter. The lesser cannot include the greater.

To me the Great Spirit is the law, the intelligence, the power which is responsible for the whole of the universe and all that it contains. That spirit is neither male nor female. That spirit is not possessed of personality, in the sense that you understand personality.

But the Great Spirit is not impersonal in the sense that you cannot reach that power. You are an essential part of the Great Spirit, as the Great Spirit is an essential part of you. In order to help to understand in some measure what is involved, we are forced to use some of your earthly expressions, but always we are conscious of the limitation of language to express what is beyond all language.

Is the Great Spirit more than an aggregate of His own creation?

Yes, with the proviso that creation is constantly expanding and an infinite process. It is not an accomplished fact. It is a fact that is always growing.

So that the Great Spirit Himself is also growing to perfection?

That part of the Great Spirit that is expressed in evolution must undergo the evolutionary processes, because infinity fills the whole universe. No part of the universe can be absent from the Great Spirit, of which it is an integral part. It is very complicated.

What settles the time of our entry into the next world? If nothing can keep us here longer than our appointed time, is this the reason why spirit healing cannot effect a cure sometimes?

Yes, it is one of the reasons. The question of spirit incarnation into matter, and what should be its natural withdrawal from matter, are governed by natural laws. You can, particularly with death, cause a premature passing, but that would not be in harmony with the natural law.

The soul itself knows when it is to be incarnated and when it is to leave your world, even though you may not be consciously aware of these facts. If it is time for the spirit to quit the body, which is inevitable as part of the law of life, then no healing—I speak generally now—can compel it to stay.

You must remember that the whole subject of spiritual healing is a highly complex one, that primarily it is designed not to heal bodies but to touch souls, and all disease has a part to play in man's unfoldment. Disease and health are necessary for the experiences of human souls. These are very controversial issues.

I cannot understand why disease should be necessary. I can see a time when man has perfected himself so that he can live a life of health without disease. If I understand you aright, disease is breaking the law.

There are always infractions of the law. If man were to live for the whole of his earthly life in perfect harmony with the law, then he would have achieved perfection on earth. You will not achieve perfection on earth because earth is imperfect.

Earth is the school where you come to learn. And you can learn only through comparison, through experiences of sunshine and shadow, of storm and peace, of love and hatred, of good and evil, of health and sickness, of well-being and pain. Only through comparison and the struggle that is entailed thereby can the soul come into its own.

Do the spirit people see us as we see each other, or can they only see our etheric body and not our physical body?

It is a good thing that we do not always see you as you see one another. We see you as spiritual beings and your body is shadowy to us, that is, unless we choose deliberately to view you through earthly eyes as when controlling a medium. Then we can view you on the physical plane because we have become physical for the time being.

Some Spiritualists talk of countless spheres in the next world. Others say there are only seven. Who is right?

The use of the word "spheres," like all attempts to define the indefinable spirit, is misleading. There are no geographical spheres. There are states of consciousness, each merging into the other as the soul evolves into deeper states of consciousness.

There is no line of demarcation, because progress, unfoldment and evolution are not determined in a series of leaps and bounds but by a very gradual sloughing off of the coarser as the more spiritual takes the forefront.

It may well be that, in early days, for the purpose of simplification, they attempted to explain that there were spheres, some corresponding to your world, some to the lower spheres than your world and others higher. But these are not arbitrary locations in space.

If pain is due to karma, what happens to the karma when the pain is relieved by spirit healing?

The questioner begs the question. If the pain is due to karma, then the pain will not be relieved until the karma is fulfilled. It cannot be any other way.

An orthodox Christian, a very good woman, has returned to a medium after death and appeals for help, saying she is living in a greyness. Why should such a good woman be living in a greyness, presumably because she never had the opportunity of learning of survival?

If the communication is genuine and she is living in

darkness or greyness, that is a reflection of her own soul-evolution. You cannot cheat the natural law and the eternal standard of goodness does not always coincide with earth's standard of goodness. Viewed with the eyes of the spirit, there are many happenings in your world which you regard as bad that we would think rather good, and many that you think are good and we think are bad.

Some churches say a man is good because he has given blind consent to some formulated doctrines, thus stifling all the essence of religion, because he can be a blackguard for the rest of his days. He is not good, though he may think he is good.

There is a fundamental goodness which has nothing to do with that standard, and it is the fundamental standard which will prevail. There are two kinds of ethics and morality. There is the morality that can be political, economic or customary, and there is the morality which is determined only by spiritual factors. It is the spiritual factor that will prevail.

What significance should a Spiritualist attach to such events as the liquefaction of blood and to stigmata?

This is largely in the realms of the individual's psyche. Faith, ardent faith, can produce through the determination of the mind the marks on the body which are equivalent to the crucifixion. It is supernormal in the sense that it is super-physical, but it does not emanate from the world of spirit.

Why should so many communicators flatly contradict each other?

You are communicating with human beings. You are not communicating with archangels who have attained to summits of wisdom. You are communicating with beings on different levels of evolution, and the information they are retailing is based on what they have experienced. They themselves will contradict some of it when later experience provides a different answer.

So many people come to our world with fixed ideas as to

what it is like. Whilst they retain their fixed ideas, it is like what they think it is. If they can express their views they do so. But there cannot be a contradiction on the fundamentals.

Many Spiritualists still cling to the idea of Jesus being part of the Godhead and the saviour of the world. Does this not clash with our Seven Principles?

I am a believer in the greatest possible tolerance and liberty, that those who think one set of words will help them should follow that path, that those who believe otherwise should follow their path. Words do not matter; doctrines are unimportant; it is only truth that counts. All of us, whether in your world or in ours, can only see very small portions of infinite truth. The more we see the more we realise there is to be seen, and the more tolerant we become.

Why does the Bible say so often, "Fear God"?

It depends on how you interpret the word "fear." It does not mean be afraid of God. It has another meaning of "reverence God."

Also would you like to comment on the part of the Lord's Prayer which says, "Lead us not into temptation"?

That is a mistranslation. There is no spirit that leads you into temptation. You do that of your own accord.

If I may make my own comment, these questions show how much farther some individuals have to go. They are bound by words, by a book and by a Church. We are not concerned with all these limitations. We are striving to make spiritual beings realise that, like the Great Spirit, they too are infinite and they must outgrow all these childish conceptions of spiritual realities.

Man must strive to master eternal truths. He cannot master them whilst he clings to shibboleths and is afraid to discard a creed, a word, a book. These may be helpful while the mind is still in the infant stage, but, as the Bible itself says, you put away childish things.

Is it possible for a developing medium to start rescue work?

It is most undesirable for such labour to be indulged in by

those who are undeveloped. Successfully to accomplish the rescue of souls in the dark or grey spheres requires the use of a highly developed instrument. If undeveloped mediums attempt the task, they may get themselves involved in obsession and many other undesirable practices.

Would you like to comment on guardian angels?

From the moment of birth into your world there is attached to every incarnating soul a spiritual being who is, in effect, the guardian angel. Sometimes this may be one who is a member of the family, in your sense of the word. At other times it may be a soul which has some affinity. But always there is a unity of interest that makes an attraction.

As to how close that association becomes is dependent upon the spiritual growth of the individual in your world. Where there is no consciousness of a guardian angel, then it is only through bringing spirit power that results can be attained.

If there is no conscious co-operation, it has to be an unconscious one. The help that comes from our world can be directed only spiritually, hoping to make its impact whenever the conditions are appropriate.

Are children born into the spirit world?

I have never seen that happen. There is birth, but this is a spiritual rebirth all the time. Children are born into your world because it is their school.

Can you say anything about the mystery of homoeopathy?

It is not a mystery, though nobody knows how anything works. We do not know how life works. We do not know the secrets of creation. We do not know how any results are achieved when you come to the fundamentals.

Homoeopathy is based in the end on a kind of spirit force; not always, but when you potentise, triturate, you come to the infinitesimal. You reach the limit and go back to the source of all life, spirit. This is the fundamental.

In other aspects it is based upon the scientific fact that attraction and reaction are equal and opposite. Similars and dissimilars are like action and reaction, opposite and equal, both ends of the same pole. Just as the Garden of Gethsemane is the end of the pole at which the Mount of Transfiguration is the top. But it is the one pole.

When people who murder others are punished by being killed, do such people receive punishment again for those actions when they pass?

Unfortunately the questioner does not possess the clue to spirit life. The whole universe is regulated by inflexible, unchanging unalterable natural laws. The law of cause and effect is a cardinal one. Effect must follow cause. Effect cannot be divorced from cause, just as cause, in itself, is the effect of a preceding cause and effect, too, becomes the cause of a proceeding effect.

Thus the natural law determines the fate of every individual, because you register your own spiritual growth. You are what you are. You cannot pretend to be what you are not. Whatever you have done in your world of matter is registered on your soul. Your soul is the richer or the poorer for that, because you have made it so.

When death parts you from your body, the soul, at the evolution it has attained, starts its new life. It cannot be higher or lower than what it is. The natural law takes cognisance of every factor. Natural law ensures that justice is done.

You punish yourself, just as you reward yourself, by every act that you perform. Man grows, or fails to grow, by his own life. That is the truth that is behind all our teaching.

From an astrological viewpoint do you confirm or refute the theory of the action of planets on human beings relative to predestination and general manner of life, bearing in mind that genuine astrology is not fortune telling?

I believe there is a planetary influence on human life in your world, but it is an influence based on a physical radiation that has more of a physical than any other effect.

I do not believe that any radiation from any planet can be

so large or potent or great that it is beyond the power of the spirit to overcome. I believe that spirit is greater than matter, that spirit is king and matter is subject.

I do not believe in predestination, in the sense that everything is predestined. It is a question of definition, of what is meant by the word. I do believe there is an ordered universe in which many important events in human life are part of the plan because they were ordained.

It is possible to measure these vibrations and radiations, and their effect on human individuals, but always I contend that the spirit is supreme, that spirit is master and that matter is the servant.

Acting on the debatable assumption that a spirit force or mind enters a future human entity on conception, where was, and what was, the activity of such spirit or mental entity on the day before the occurrence of the event?

Leaving aside all questions of reincarnation, on the day before the entry of spirit into matter it existed, but not in personalised form. It is in the association of spirit and matter that personality begins to develop, and, concurrently with its development, the innate individuality begins to express itself.

The answer is that spirit always has existed but does not become individuated until it starts its association with the body of matter. There are many exceptions to that in the case of souls who are not incarnated for the first time.

If that is so, and spirit has no individuality, how is it then directed to its new task of associating with matter?

You have to draw a distinction between personality and individuality. Personality is the earthly aspect of individuality, which is the eternal possession. As individuality, the spirit always has existence, but it cannot make that existence known on earth except through personality. Personality is the bodily form through which individuality is expressed. It is the mask, not the real wearer. It is the earthly expression, the outward expression of an inner reality.

So if people are reincarnated, is the purpose to acquire greater personality and not individuality?

Not necessarily, it can be that what is incarnated is another fragment of that individuality which attains the necessary experience through earthly life to help in the unfoldment of the larger individuality of which it is a part. Individuality is much larger in spirit sense than any understanding of it that you have in your world.

Do you know of anyone who has reincarnated back to this planet?

Yes, many, but I could not prove it to you. You must take my word for it, or reject it, it does not matter. Truth is not affected by anybody's opinion of it.

How should one bred in the Christian tradition, but anxious to learn the truth, look upon Christ?

Here again it is a question of what is meant by the words that are used. It is very difficult for people who are bred in any religious tradition to face such problems with impartiality because they are unconsciously prejudiced before they begin.

The word "Christ" means "the anointed" and there have been many who were anointed. If the questioner is referring to the Nazarene, then his attitude should be one of respect for a being who came to show the way spiritually, psychically and physically according to the time in which he lived.

But this being was not the Great Spirit, and the Great Spirit was not this being. If the theological interpretation is accepted that it was the Great Spirit taking physical form, then the whole value of the Nazarene's life is lost and meaningless.

It would be easy for the Great Spirit to take human form and live almost a perfect, blameless life, but if a human being, born according to the ordinary, natural laws, shows what can be achieved, that is a worthy example for all to follow.

Revelation is not unique at any time, in any country, or in any language. There is only one source of all revelation, the infinite store-house. In every age attempts have been made to flood the world with that amount of wisdom and inspiration and knowledge suited to the conditions of the people who dwell together.

You should not turn only to the past. You should realise that now, wherever you are, you have access to the eternal fount of all inspiration.

Arising out of that, I think you said it would be fairly simple for the Great Spirit to live an earthly life. Doesn't that rather lead to the view that God is a person?

If the question is based on the premise that God Himself took human shape, is the first, or second, or third portion of a trinity, then the perfect God could easily lead a perfect life. There is no virtue in it. The whole point of the Nazarene's mission disappears.

I am not suggesting that the Great Spirit is a human figure. The Great Spirit is beyond all human personality, but attempts to convey the Great Spirit can be conveyed only in language that is understandable to human beings with human limitations.

Who was Jesus of Nazareth? Was he a man with unusual psychic gifts who was controlled by his guide in all that he said and did, or was he the reincarnation of some highly evolved spirit?

Both are true. You must remember that you have limited knowledge of that life because the records are meagre, have not been free from tampering and are very fragmentary.

The great value in that life is that here was an example of how psychic and spiritual power could be used. The Nazarene never contradicted or took advantage of any psychic or spiritual law. He was the master of these in his understanding of their operation though his humanity sometimes came to the foremost.

Historically the figure came at a time when it was necessary for this revelation to illumine the world. This illumination was performed with that same power of the spirit that is operating in your midst today.

When meditating or submitting to the world of spirit i.e. developing psychic or spiritual faculties, how can we attract only sincere spirits and how can we repel the forces of evil?

Like attracts like. If you motive is sincere, if your aspiration is to reach out to the highest, if there is no evil in your own thought, if you desire nothing for yourself, then by the very law of attraction those of equal desires assist and no possible harm can befall you.

The very atmosphere that pervades you makes it impossible for any but those of like-minded desires to reach you. If the saint could attract the foolish ones in our world, it would make nonsense of the laws of the universe.

You tell us that our spirit loved ones are always with us. But is a part of their personality free in the spirit world?

Yes they can be with you and enjoy the beauties of our world at the same time, because they are not bound to a body such as you possess. Consciousness, when it expresses in our life, is not restricted as you are in your world. You cannot be in England and South Africa at the same time, but we can because we are not subject to the problems of distance or travel that you have.

It is no hardship on those who love you to be with you. If they did not love you, then they would not stay with you. Because they love you they would rather keep with you than wander away.

Is a spirit guide always used for spirit help, rather than the direct intervention of the Great Spirit?

There is no such thing as direct intervention by the Great Spirit because the Great Spirit is not personal in the sense that you understand personality. The Great Spirit is law, the Great Spirit is love, the Great Spirit is wisdom.

But there are countless intermediaries, beings on every rung of the Jacob's ladder that ranges from the lowest to the highest. Those on the higher rungs are more qualified to express the divine will and wisdom than the lower ones.

Thus, as man opens up, unfolds, reaches out, he makes himself more accessible to the higher beings who have greater power, greater knowledge, greater understanding. They are all servants of the Great Spirit, all voluntarily working in the great task of helping humanity throughout the whole of the universe. The more evolved you become in our life the more you realise that whatever you have gained you should strive to offer to others. I think that answers the question.

Have you ever heard of the halls of learning in the spirit world?

Of course I have. Our systems of enlightenment are quite simple. We have halls, colleges and universities where every aspect of knowledge is available. The teachers qualified to give tuition are those who are endowed by their gifts to do so.

There is knowledge available on every subject in an infinite universe and there are teachers in qualifying degrees to expound this knowledge to those who are ready to receive it. It matters not what aspects of knowledge is desired, it is available for who is ready to receive it. The qualifying phrase is the readiness of the soul.

It is possible for people in our world to have access to information on any aspect of learning. It is quite a simple matter to obtain information on subjects that interest you, or that are helpful to your progress, unfoldment or development.

Which is the greater service, the one given through love or that given through devotion to duty?

It depends on the service that is rendered. It can be answered by seeking its motive—and you would have to explain what you meant by love. Love in its highest form is divine; love in its lowest form is the acme of selfishness.

All service is service. The measure of its worth is the effect on the one who is served and its reaction on the server. If it is caused by devotion to duty, that is admirable. If it is caused by true love that is unselfish and does not desire only to help the object of affection, then it is a worthy motive too.

Apart from healing, has the Spiritualist movement grown beyond the need for physical phenomena?

No, there is always a need because of those who must see and touch, who must have the evidence on their own material plane.

This includes not only the materialist but the scientist who, by his training, cannot accept as truth that which is outside the bounds of the five senses. There may be changes in the forms of phenomena, but there will always be some demonstration of the physical aspects, which will come and go in successive waves.

Would it not be more evidential if public clairvoyants also gave the name of the recipient of spirit messages instead of merely indicating the person?

Of course it would be, but, as it says in your Bible, we see and hear only in part. The questioner does not realise that all mediumship is experimental due to the conditions prevailing at the time—the state of awareness the medium's soul has reached the stage of unfoldment that their psychic powers have reached, the ability of the communicator to register within the aura of the medium and the amount of unity that exists between the medium and the guide.

All these factors are at work when clairvoyance is being given. It is not a question of what should be done. It is a question of the best that can be done at the time.

A sitter commented: "You have said something akin to this, that in embryo, in miniature, in microcosm, you are part of the Great Spirit." Silver Birch agreed, saying: "You are the God or the Great Spirit and the Great Spirit is you. It is all a matter of degree. The Great Spirit does not possess any quality that you do not possess in essence. The Great Spirit is divine; you are divine. It is a difference of degree; it is not a difference of the inherent quality of divinity."

Where there are mental cases suffering great pain, who cannot express themselves, would it not be better for them to pass on?

Who is to decide when they shall be put to death? Who is to take the responsibility? Who is to say when it is impossible ever for that individual to regain sanity? Cannot some awakening take place that will restore the right relationship and banish the illness of the mind or spirit?

I do not agree with these ideas. You do not create life; do not attempt to end it. They should live their allotted span which is necessary to equip the soul with the experience it requires for the next stage of evolution. To attempt to assess infinity by a material fragment is to take a very poor and jaundiced view of an infinite universe.

Leading from that, would it be possible for the soul to lose qualities rather than gain them?

No, it cannot lose them. It can be undeveloped because it cannot express itself, but it cannot lose its inherent qualities. They will, by virtue of the law of compensation, be able to express themselves in other ways that would not otherwise be possible.

Why do not spirit communicators use simple language, as we are led to believe that simplicity is an attribute of God? They always speak with indirect allusions to all who are their superiors in spirit life. We speak of God on earth, but they speak not of God, but of the Great White Spirit.

It is not always easy to be simple when you are dealing with subjects that are complex and profound. You call it God, I call it the Great White Spirit. What is the difference?

To me the Great White Spirit gives a better idea of the power that is behind the universe than the word God which means entirely different things to millions of people. Simplicity is a virtue when it can be achieved and I do not think that, so far as I am concerned, I can be accused of avoiding simplicity.

It is not easy to convey ideas of the superior beings in spirit life. For me there is no comparison in your world. You who are familiar with beings like yourself will find it very hard to understand some of the greater souls with whom occasionally it is our privilege to establish communication.

How can you convey a being who is nearly all light to those who visualise a being as possessing a certain human shape? It is not possible, in your language, to match the reality which it tries to convey. It is not from any desire of concealment, but simply because the state of evolution that your world has reached is not high enough for it to appreciate stages that are infinitely superior to its own.

Would it be possible for me to form a circle where you could answer questions?

We seem to have anticipated it here. I am very grateful for the implied compliment, but it has taken me many years to develop an instrument suitable for this purpose. I do not see that it is part of a plan that I should spend another long period of training when the purpose is already achieved.

I wish to become clairvoyant, but so far this has eluded me. Is this due to eagerness?

Eagerness can be too much of a deterrent, because it sets up vibrations which disturb the atmosphere. The best development, whether of the psychic or of the inner spiritual faculties, is achieved when there is complete passivity, peace and quietude.

Is there any spiritual implication involved when a person gives blood as a blood donor, and does it affect any but the physical body?

I must repeat by disagreement with the idea of blood transfusion. It is not only the blood which is transferred but the accompanying etheric counterpart, which is part of the individual from whom it is taken. It is not only blood that is being given but the conditions that appertain to the essence of the being, and that is not always desirable.

Man is a complex whole, in which every aspect of his being dovetails as part of the intricate mechanism. It is not intended that one part should be transferred to another person, because it is upsetting a natural harmony which should exist in the right relationship between body, mind and spirit.

There does seem to be some evidence that lives are saved by it.

I would not say anything that would appear to detract from the value of work that is done in any sphere to heal the sick, but I would put in one word of criticism, that is the assumption that any current medical practice represents the only means by which the results can be achieved.

There is a tendency to ascribe infallibility to your medical world, and if its representatives assert that this is the method by which a cure can be obtained, or life prolonged, that must of necessity be the last word on the subject. I do not subscribe to such views.

I would say that there are countless means of healing all based on one principle, that man is a spiritual being and that all healing is directed to the end that the spirit shall triumph. The body exists only because it is the machine for the spirit.

It may well be that these are the means by which life can be saved, but it is very questionable that in other directions you should resort to odious and horrible and unspiritual practices with the intent of saving what you call life.

Do you mean vivisection?

Yes. The end does not justify the means.

What about grafting?

If it is done from your own body, all well and good, because the self-same properties, material and etheric, are at work, but when it is transferred to anyone else, it is not always satisfactory because of what you are transferring. Once you realise that matter has no existence of itself, that it is only a shell or the coat of an invisible reality that you call spirit, you have the key to the whole situation.

Is it desired that a person should remain blind when grafting would give sight again?

It is very difficult to answer generally questions without knowing the individual conditions, but physical blindness is comparative. What about spiritual blindness?

We have to look down on millions who are spiritually

blind. That is why I answer your question and say it depends on the condition of the soul. If the individual had obtained heights of spiritual understanding then physical blindness would be no handicap. He would have a sight that is far greater than your physical eyes could achieve. Always you look at the problems from the standpoint of your physical body and not from eternity, and I do not blame you for so doing.

But without eyes we would miss the spring and the flowers.

The glories of the spring, the beauty of the flowers and the wonder of sunshine pale into insignificance compared with the glories and the radiance of the spirit.

But we are still in this world.

Yes, and you should know that you can be in this world and not of this world.

'To help the unfortunate'

OH Great White Spirit, Though who art the infinite architect, the king of kings, the divine intelligence which has devised the whole universal scheme, whose wisdom sustains it and whose love guides it, we seek to draw close to Thee, to garner from Thy infinite storehouse of knowledge some gleanings that will aid us on our eternal quest.

We recognise that we cannot understand Thee in Thy fullness because Though art infinite and our conceptions must of necessity be finite ones.

We see the panorama of natural laws unfolding in the immensity of their gigantic scope, controlling all facets of life in a boundless universe.

We know that Thou art not the jealous, despotic tyrant that men have taught, but Thou art the infinite intelligence, with favours for none and with curses for none.

Thou has instituted the laws that control all life so that cause and effect follow one another in unalterable and unbreakable sequence.

Those who draw close to Thee, who are in harmony with Thee and who express Thy will, reap the result in lives of serenity and confidence, in lives filled with lustre and richness.

And those who have not found Thee, alas, are lost in the mists of darkness and ignorance, surrounded always by shadows that obscure their path.

It is part of our task, all of us who yearn to serve mankind, to help the unfortunate, the needy, the broken-hearted mourner, the sick persons, the ones in despair and doubt and difficulty, those whose backs are heavy with the load that they have to carry, those who have lost their way and do not know where to turn.

It is our desire to help them to find that truth which will act as a lighthouse to guide them on their path. We express our gratitude that the power of the spirit is able to manifest itself in increasing strength through many instruments whose desire is to bring the richness of divine truth and wisdom to those whose souls are ready for it.

Touched by the power of the spirit, and with those magnetic links forged, the whole of their lives will be lived in the fullness which is part of their divine heritage.

Thus, gradually, but increasingly, mankind will turn its back on chaos, on selfishness, on greed and on war.

And as the power of the spirit finds a greater expression in the lives of increasing numbers, so peace will make its way and the kingdom of heaven on earth become a reality.

To this end we pray and direct all our labours.

Chapter 8

'THE RIDDLE OF LIFE'

"How far is it proper to ask for help in one's daily life from spirit guides and friends?" The question was put to Silver Birch by a businessman, a convinced Spiritualist. The guide told him: "We who attach ourselves to earthly instruments have to become very familiar with the needs and habits and demands of your world. We cannot be immune to material necessities, for we have to deal with beings who live in your world.

After all, matter and spirit are both servants of the Great Spirit, and the temple of the spirit has certain necessities, requires certain attention and must perform certain duties so as to be able to fulfil its place in the great scheme.

Your bodies require light, air, shelter, clothing and food. To do this you must have money, the coin of your world. I know all that, but I know this, too.

Matter is the servant, spirit is the master. Those who reverse that order make a great mistake. By virtue of your spiritual nature, which is your aspect of divinity, you possess in miniature all that the Great Spirit possesses.

The great, creative principles which enable life to fulfil its functions are possessed by you. You are the Great Spirit, the Great Spirit is you, and within you, by virtue of your birth, there is all the armoury of the Great Spirit.

The power that fashioned all life and is responsible for the working of every phase of the universe resides within you. You can tap it, you can draw on this inexhaustible reservoir.

If you learn to be still, you can allow its great immeasurable force to come into being, and because it is spiritual it is able to overcome all the difficulties, all the problems with which you are confronted. Added to that you have the love and guidance of those close to you from our world.

Whenever a difficulty arises, become passive. Let there well up within you from your own infinite store, albeit it is not yet completely expressed, the answer that is waiting. It will come.

If by virtue of development, for we are all creatures of evolution, the answer is not forthcoming, then pause again and, instead of coming from within, it will come from without.

Right and wrong, these are words; what concerns us is motive. With all requests with all prayers, the paramount consideration is motive.

If the motive is sincere, if the desire is to serve, if there is an ideal to be attained, if unselfishness and altruism are the guiding principles, then he or she who asks for help cannot be refused.

By virtue of their own state of evolution, they are already putting into motion that which will produce the answer to their prayers.

When a member of the circle said that some of the best and most conscientious men worried, the guide commented:

Are you not confusing purely physical attainment with spiritual knowledge? If they are the possessors of knowledge of spiritual realities, they must know there is no need to worry. You can go through life conscientiously discharging your duties without worrying about them.

I do not mean you should be indifferent to your obligations; that is not part of my teaching. Rather do we stress that you shall become more conscious of them. But there is no need to worry. There can be mental development which is not parallel with spiritual growth.

The same member of the circle said, "To put it plainly, anyone who worries is not spiritually developed."

Yes, it is so. The saints never worry because they are conscious of the Great Plan. You can have a good mind and be an honest, charitably disposed individual, quite unselfish, and still not have attained those soul-qualities that bring you a close awareness of the meaning and purpose of life.

The teaching that says there is a contrary happening to that inexorable law is wrong. There can be no intervention between cause and effect.

There are no means by which the responsibilities of your actions can be transferred to other shoulders, neither can the responsibility of the actions of others be transferred to your shoulders. Each must carry the burden of his own life. That is honest, moral, ethical and just.

All else is debased, cowardly, immoral and unjust. The law is perfect.

In perhaps an esoteric way, are we not responsible for everybody else, because if we try to make the world a better place we are responsible.

Yes, in that sense we are responsible. We are our brothers' keepers because the thread of spirit runs throughout all humanity and binds us together to make us one. But our responsibility is to ensure that we help and serve and co-operate to the fullness of our knowledge.

Our responsiblity ends with what others do with their lives. But none lives by himself alone; we are all inter-dependent on one another. All life mingles and merges and blends and harmonises. All of us live together in one universe and our actions affect others.

That is why knowledge brings great responsibility. He who sins without knowledge is not so bad as he who sins with knowledge, for the sin has been increased by the awareness of the action. It is no light task to embark on a spiritual quest, for knowledge brings the capacity for greater responsiblity.

Sorrow and happiness, these are equally servants of the Great Spirit. You cannot have one without the other. As high as you can reach, so low can you fall, and as low as you can fall, so high can you reach. It must be so.

Fear is an instinctive element in our being. How in fact can we abolish it? It is a mechanism used by nature to safeguard her creatures. The natural animal world is full of fear. If fear is contrary to all reason, why is it part of the very warp and weft of the animal kingdom?

I think that is a very good question. Man is a duality and in his existence he expresses not only the remains of his animal ancestry but the divine spirit which is his natural heritage. And he is given the blessed gift of free will to help him in his evolutionary path to tread the higher way, because in doing so the divinity within him will find expression.

Thus he possesses always the eternal choice as to whether he will use his growing powers for selfish or unselfish purposes. If he gives way to that which was implanted within him because his body has come right from primeval beginnings through all its evolutionary shapes to what it is today, then he is denying the supremacy of the spirit which gives him the breath to live in this world.

All fear is largely due to that animal ancestry. And when I say the animal ancestry, I include all the aspects of evolution through which the body has passed. But it is not always a rational fear. There is the fear which activates self-protection, but there is the irrational fear which is blank and hopeless, which exaggerates difficulty and danger and which blinds because it is unaware of the spiritual realities on which all life must be founded.

Doesn't it mean that an animal by its nature must always have fear?

Man is expressing a much higher consciousness than any animal and therefore he should be able to control his mental processes, whereas, with the exception of domestic animals, other creatures are behaving instinctively. Man is endowed with the power of reason. He has the ability to be inspired by higher forces from a larger life and to utilise wisdom and knowledge to banish all that belongs to the darkness and ignorance.

Even animals as they evolve do not have such fear. They are naturally afraid of man because of mistreatment.

That is what I said. You must except the domestic animals which now, through association with man, begin to absorb some of that consciousness, to become individuals themselves and to learn to abolish fear. It is the power of love in action. As man displays love, so it drives out all fear. You must remember that man in his free will is responsible for instilling into many animals a fear which is not normal to them, and often what you call wild creatures, confronted with love, will abolish fear. And truly the lion and the lamb can dwell together.

If, as you say, the law is perfect in its operation and works with an unfailing mathematical exactitude, takes account of every cognisance and provides a perfect balance so that no soul is unjustly treated, then by implication do you expound karmic law and reincarnation as truths.

The short answer is yes.

I read that doctors stopped a heart beating for 15 minutes to perform a delicate operation. I thought the spirit left the body immediately the heart ceased to beat.

The heart begins to stop beating when the spirit begins to withdraw itself. But the process of withdrawal takes a long time usually, that is when death is natural. Sometimes there are automatic reactions, purely mechanical, and sometimes through defective mechanism there may be pauses in the beating of the heart, even though the spirit has not withdrawn. But it is not that stopping of the heart beat expels the spirit, it is the other way round. When spirit withdraws then the beating ceases to function.

As using atomic energy for even constructive purposes depends on breaking the atom, is such action a violation of the natural law of harmony and so a danger to humanity?

This is a very difficult question because it involves many things which your world cannot yet understand. There is a law of harmony in the universe which you can disturb, but you cannot break or change the expression of natural law. By that I mean very simply that if it were impossible to split the atom then you could not do so.

What is certainly true is that this is a discovery out of its natural evolution, that is, something that is really before its time, something for which your world is not yet mentally or spiritually ready. If it were, then problems of the use of atomic energy would simply not exist. Man, because of this discovery, has had access to power for which he is not spiritually ready and because of that may do great harm. It will resolve itself as and when true wisdom guides those who hold the destiny of earthly nations in their power.

From childhood we are brought up to believe in God as a God of Love and as our Heavenly Father. Is it then conceivable that spirit entities who have finished with their earth life can obsess us who are here?

Yes, of course, they can.

And that those who are here can be permitted by God to be obsessed?

The Great Spirit is a law; it is not an individual who issues permits for things to happen in a universe in which the law of cause and effect operates. You cannot have laws controlling communication and say that these will be used only by good people. The same channels are available to the selfish and the unselfish.

If people live the kind of life on earth that makes them earth-bound afterwards, the Great Spirit cannot be blamed for their selfishness, greed and avarice. And if, as a result, there are people equally as selfish who lay themselves open to be obsessed because of their foolish habits of drugs and drink and greed, why blame the Great Spirit for what they have done of their own free will?

Is it part of the spirit plan that healing occupies its foremost position today?

The answer is an unequivocal yes. It is part of the plan that the power of the spirit shall be made manifest in the healing of the sick, thus demonstrating that there is a divine power used through instruments that can bring healing to those for whom life was bleak and drear and desolate.

The power of the spirit, part of the life-force itself, part of the infinite spirit streaming through countless channels, is able to vitalise and infuse new energies into bodies that have been so racked and tortured by disease and affliction that when results are achieved, even the most critical and sceptical have to admit that this is a power which cannot be explained in human or earthly terms. It is part of the plan because it supplies the need which is suited to the time in which you live.

Why are spirit agencies dependent on an invitation before they heal?

Because until a request is made an answer cannot be given. The spirit power for healing has to be called into being. The life-force is circulating throughout the whole universe in all its manifestations as part of its universal activity, but if you want some aspect of that power to reach an individual, until the request is made that it should do so, there is no intelligence applied to the direction of the force.

Cannot the intelligence come from your side?

Yes it does, but until it has a means of expressing itself, it is entirely spiritual and operating only on a spiritual plane. To be effective in your world, there must be a medium, a nexus, a channel, an instrument through which spirit power can flow to reach someone.

It is the same as asking if you are separated from your wife, why does she not telephone you without a telephone. It is only when there is a means by which she can reach you that she can reach you.

Why must this invitation be addressed to the medium?

It must be so because the medium is the focus. The other aspect of the question is that when the appeal is made for spiritual help, it is a sign that the soul is beginning to come into its own and is aware that spiritual help can be given. And, as you know, the whole purpose of healing, like every other aspect of our activity, is to focus attention on man's own spiritual nature.

And that awakening in part attracts healing to itself?

Yes, because the soul coming into its own automatically is able to attract forces to which it is naturally allied.

Is that the explanation of the worlds, "Ask and ye shall receive"?

Yes, of course. When you ask, you set in motion the desire of the soul to be satisfied and that is setting the links in the chain working by which the power comes to you, by which the answers come.

Why should one medium be more spectacularly successful than another since all healers presumably direct the same influence to their patients?

The power of the spirit has an infinite number of manifestations, and what can be expressed through any particular channel is dependent upon the qualities of that instrument, physically, mentally and spiritually. Their temperaments, their states of evolution, their character, their outlook, all these are factors which qualify the type and amount of spirit power that can function through them. In essence it is one power, but, like truth, it has countless facets.

Can the patient's attitude affect the efficacy of the cure?

Yes, of course. The spirit power must work according to the operation of natural laws. These laws control the ebb and flow of the power, and they are subject to a variety of conditions that are spiritual, mental and physical. Not only do these obtain so far as the healer is concerned, they must obtain so far as the patient is concerned.

I know that you can quote cases of healing at a distance when it has been achieved without the knowledge of the patient, but I would remind you that although it may be without his conscious knowledge it is not without the knowledge of his soul, which is the part that is treated. All spiritual healing works from within to without.

Can you explain the modus operandi of absent healing?

I do not see in a world which is familiar with the reality of the invisible, the intangible and the inaudible that it should find difficulty in understanding how spiritual radiations can find their target. You have now a variety of instruments and appliances which demonstrate with unerring accuracy that vibrations, though unseen to you, can be made visible and that they obey certain well-defined laws. In absent healing definite vibrations, or radiations, of force, power, or rays—the labels do not matter—are used, and these are directed by intelligence to the instruments.

Have we all the power to heal ourselves?

Inherently yes, because being spirit, part of the Great Spirit, we have the life-force, the vital spark, the dynamic, as an integral part of our being. Thus there is within us, as part of us, that which enables life to function. If you could understand the means by which it can be expressed, then this power could be used to heal yourself.

Healing overcomes suffering, yet we are told that we must suffer on earth to learn the lessons of life. If this is so, does not healing rob us of the opportunity and act as a barrier to spiritual development?

Nothing can interfere with the operation of natural law. The universe is directed by infinite intelligence which is unfailing and unerring in all that it does. Nothing can short-circuit these manifestations of natural law. There is a great deal of suffering, but often this is unnecessary suffering caused by foolish transgression of the law. The purpose of earthly life is to develop the spirit and there is a variety of methods by which this purpose is achieved. Suffering is one of them, but it is not the only way.

What is the difference between the various types of healing, such as faith healing, spirit healing, magnetic healing, divine healing, etc.?

Broadly, I would say that healing falls into two categories—the healing that operates from spirit, and the healing that operates from the incarnate spirit in your world. The mesmeric, the magnetic and the hypnotic, and auto-suggestion, all these are part of the healing due to the incarnate spirit at work and need not have any association with our world, just as individuals can express their psychic faculties without any touch with the world of spirit.

The other kind of healing emanates from our world and has a variety of expressions called many names because different aspects are involved. But whatever form the healing takes and whatever label is used the basis is always spirit power at work.

What steps can a healing medium take to become an even better instrument?

Spend your life in the desire to serve, seeking no thought of self, desiring only to help others. That predominating aspiration is the best factor in the development of any gift of the spirit. That will make the healer love not only those who suffer but the whole of humanity, and in that love the power to heal must increase.

Why does a healer catch cold, go down with the flu and become a prey to minor ailments?

Because he has trangressed the law and has to pay the price. Like everybody else, a healer, though he is an instrument of spirit power, is not immune from the operation of natural law. There is no magic: the law works quite naturally and if healers transgress it, they must face the consequences.

Why is it that many healers cannot cure themselves?

In most cases the healer is an instrument through which the spirit power flows. He is transmitting, and his reception is only for the purpose of transmission. There are many healers who can heal themselves, but if the power streams through their instrumentality, it may not necessarily have any of it deflected to the purpose of self-healing. It depends on the type of channel.

If a healer, for example, has some accident to the physical body that impairs its functioning and it does not prevent him from performing his healing to others, he may decide that what happens to his own defect is unimportant. I think I would so decide if I could heal others.

Are healers wrong in assuming that because they are healers they are automatically helped without asking?

Healing is a positive, not a negative, factor. Healing is achieved from an awareness of the soul. The soul must come into its own. It is a question of vibration. When the soul comes into its own it desires to burst the barriers. It is demanding and seeking, and it is that which should be expressed.

When people lose a dearly loved one, they look forward with great joy to the reunion. What happens to people like the writer who has not had anybody to love?

The laws of the Great Spirit are perfect in their operation. "Through millions of years they have unceasingly been at work without failure. In the vast cosmic scheme nothing has been overlooked or forgotten, neither is this soul outside the scope of the natural laws. These laws provide compensation, so that whatever lacks in your world is fully supplied in ours. The perfect balance is always struck and the laws fulfil themselves. No one ever gets forgotten in the divine scheme.

Are yoga discipline and body control essential to full spiritual development? Are they even helpful to anybody?

The answer to the first part of the question is that they are not essential. They are methods of disciplining the body, instilling self-mastery, demonstrating the control of mind over matter. By doing so, naturally you encourage the growth of your psychic powers, but they are not essential. There are other roads of attainment. I must say that I think this form of discipline is more suited to the eastern than to your western world.

Why do you say that?

Because by nature they are more contemplative and more interested in meditation. They have atmospheric conditions to help to acclimatise them. They are well versed in religious ideas in which this kind of happening has been in the forefront in the lives of their leaders.

It is probably true to say there is some other equivalent discipline we ought to follow?

I am a great believer in the discipline which teaches the mind to demonstrate its control over the body, in so far as it leads to release of the spiritual nature. But it does not necessarily follow that because you can suspend your breathing, or control the pulse rate, or the flow of blood, that you are a better person spiritually.

If it is not too wide a question, what sort of discipline should a western man use?

The silence. I am one of those who believe that you should set aside a little time each day to retire into the silence of your home and your soul, to allow the power of the spirit to rise to the surface. You are so busy in your world that you have little time for spiritual refreshment. It is only when you are quiet, receptive and subdued, that the spiritual forces within and without can manifest.

Is the sleep-state any good?

Not for the active and positive development of the spiritual nature. The sleep-state is part of the natural function by which your spirit body is released to familiarise itself with our world and to prepare for your future habitation.

Many people on the point of death say that they have seen a vision of Jesus. The Pope has now said he has seen a vision of Jesus. Who or what was this vision?

That is a very interesting question, but of course, it is impossible to verify what people see in visions. It does not of necessity follow that a vision is an appearance of an individual. In our world you cannot show yourself to people on earth in physical form. Therefore you can only show yourself in pictorial form.

I cannot show you myself as I am because you have no means of cognising the form in which I naturally express myself. The Nazarene cannot show himself, in the form in which he now manifests, to people in your world because there is no bridge on which they can meet. All that can be shown is a picture for them to comprehend.

A picture of the Nazarene in his present form would mean nothing to his most ardent disciple in your world today. Those who see visions are not looking at reality, in the sense that they are seeing the individual whom they think is portrayed in their vision, but they are seeing the pictorial representation. Does that help them?

Could it be a projection of their own thought?

Yes, sometimes if it is strong enough to materialise in the form of a picture, because their own mentality has the latent power to build pictures. If you are prepared to hold the thoughts so intensively on their own plane, they will take shape. These are not physical appearances. The visions must be etheric, spiritual, astral, psychic, or on one of the levels of the non-physical world.

Is it true also that because of the fact that they are on the point of death they can see more?

There are two facts to be borne into consideration. There is no one in your world who knows what the Nazarene looks like now. Still less do they know what he looked like in the days when he trod the earth, so that they have no means of saying that this is a vision of the Nazarene.

At the moment of death a tremendous amount of psychic and spiritual energy becomes released. That is why you have so many cases of people who, when they are passing to our world, are able to manifest to relatives many miles away from them. That burst of psychic and spiritual energy carries them and, still only being so close to earth, although they have passed, they are able almost to materialise themselves. But it happens only at the moment of their passing. Similarly with those having visions, it can be the outcome of their own release of psychic and spiritual energy.

Some say there is no hell. What are the dark and twilight regions if there is no hell?

There is a hell, although it does not follow the conventional pictures. Of course there are the darker spheres where the undeveloped souls live, and these regions are certainly hell for those who live in them. It is a reality. If you think of the people who have plunged the world into darkness and misery, who have caused needless bloodshed—what do you think is the sort of life they have in our world?

It is not heaven for them when they are confronted with the results of what they have done. Of course there is a hell, not with fire and brimstone, but the hell of the soul that meets itself face to face, that realises its own wickedness, its own evil, its own selfishness. That is hell, and it is far more damning to the soul than any of the conceptions painted by mediæval artists.

What happens to our guides after we have passed over? Is their work with us finished the moment we return to the spirit world?

If the purpose of the association was for work in your world, then obviously that association ends with the instrument passing, because the work has been done. The function of a guide is to use an instrument to develop his or her psychic faculties so that they can be utilised for service. That surely ends with the passing of the instrument.

It is rather a sad thought to some of us who have learned to love the guides that there is no link afterwards.

I said the association was over, but that does not mean to say that there would be separation. So far as the world is concerned, the mission comes to an end.

I think that is what the person meant.

As to whether she will meet them, of course she will.

Would any special relationship continue?

Not if it is only the relationship of guide and instrument, because the work is finished.

It does not mean they will not see each other.

As you have heard me say so many times, the answer must be qualified because there are degrees of relationship between guides and instruments and you touch aspects of consciousness and individuality which refer to larger subjects.

You want to know whether you will see me and whether I will see my instrument. Of course we shall meet, but I will not be speaking like this, I hope.

When endeavouring to obtain results for the direct voice or other physical phenomena what should be the mental attitude of the sitters? Should they allow trance, clairvoyance and clairaudience to occur? If not can these forms of manifestation be controlled while sitting for the development of physical mediumship? If so, how?

When individuals desire physical phenomena, to encourage mental phenomena obviously would be a deterrent. They should discourage any attempts at clairvoyance, clairaudience and trance and say they would prefer to wait patiently while the other gifts which would produce physical results are unfolded.

Can these forms of physical manifestation be controlled? What should be the technique to stop them?

It merely means that those who possess latent gifts for mental phenomena should not open themselves out. If my instrument does not allow me to come through I cannot do it, but as he places himself in the receptive mind, it makes it easy for me to enter.

Another questioner asked whether it was advisable to join the Freemasons.

It is not by joining any order, or group, or body that matters, it is what the individual does that counts. If by joining any association the individual is encouraged to lead a life that is more kindly, more unselfish, more altruistic, one that is of service to others, then let him join.

But always the acid test, the only test, is the way he conducts his own life. He will have to bear the burden of everything that he does.

A sitter asked the guide whether he considered the teachings of Freemasonry to be of benefit in the development of psychic gifts.

They are beneficial to those who understand the significance of them and realise that what others regard as symbols are in reality part of psychic unfoldment.

Is it a good thing for what are really secret societies to flourish? Should not truth be open to everybody? It should not be cornered by a few.

No, the truth cannot be cornered, because truth is boundless and none can set a limit to it. It does not matter whether these things are done in secret or not, if the motive is to do good. You must judge always by the motive. It is what the individual does with his life that counts.

We have returned to make religion a very practical matter. No longer is it to be relegated to beliefs or forms or ceremonies. Instead we assert with all the force at our command that religion is a matter of service and everything which encourages the individual to serve is good.

Freemasons largely confine their service to people who are also in the order.

I know, but at least some service is being rendered and a start is being made.

Is it true, as some mediums state, that there is a place for suicides? Some mediums say they have seen these places and they are such that they cannot contemplate.

It is true in a certain sense that the clairvoyant vision may have seen one sphere or plane of spirit life where those who have cut short their earthly existence have congregated because that is the level of their attainment.

But it is not true in the sense that there is one fixed place for all who have committed suicide.

Each case is determined by what it is. The law, the unfailing law, operates in every instance. As I have said so many times, the factor which determines the whole situation is the one of motive, for that is the index to the soul of the individual.

Some are on the same level, in the same way as some are on the same level as far as religious bigotry is concerned, and you find groups of them. You go to the place for which you are fitted.

A sitter suggested that suicides would have a common interest which might, to some extent, draw them together.

They must be on the same spiritual level because that determines where they are. What you are spiritually governs where you are spiritually because our world is a world in which spiritual states are translated into reality.

Some suicides are on the same plane. That is why I said a clairvoyant vision could reveal a sphere or plane where a group would be.

The next question was contained in a letter which read, "We believe that our mental life passes with us. What is the state of those who pass over 'out of their minds,' in particular those cases who have suffered long years of insanity?"

If you have been mentally deranged, it means that your mind has not had the opportunity to reach the full development which is the purpose of earthly life. The mind will not be destroyed. It will be impaired, but all its faculties will be intact, albeit undeveloped.

In such cases the individual passes to our world with the mentality of a child and gradually adjustment is made so that this lack of development is rectified. There is no permanent injury to the spirit. It is a temporary condition, not permanent, and can soon be adjusted.

Why do our loved ones on their return not tell us of their interests, studies, and those whom they have met and how they have progressed?

Why are the usual messages just a few odd names, some flowers, a statement that all will be well with us shortly, and that they are with us and helping us. Why not news such as we should write if we were on holiday?

It is not quite the same, is it? If the whole process of communication with your world were as simple as sending a letter while you were on holiday, a great deal more information would be forthcoming, but unfortunately it is far more complicated than sending a letter.

Initially, communication is limited to fragments. When you have a chance to utter perhaps a sentence or two, naturally you desire to assure those left behind that all is well. That is a great message, and it means so much to those who hear it for the first time.

But I must differ from the one who asks the question when it is suggested that when the channel is open the communication is limited to the fragments with which it begins. Again and again, vast information has been transmitted and this is to be found recorded in many books.

'From the stars that swing'

LET us strive by harmony and love to attune ourselves to the highest that we can reach. Let us so banish all thoughts of care and anxiety and, allowing our souls to rise to the surface, approach the Author of all being, the Lord of all creation, and ask the Great White Spirit to give us the benediction of His power and His glory.

Oh Great White Spirit, we who are Thy children and who are made in the divine mould, approach Thee in reverence and sincerity and earnestness, desiring to glean further wisdom to add to our little store.

We have learned much that has dissipated the misconceptions of Thee and brought us closer to Thou who art the infinite spirit, whose wondrous laws control, regulate and sustain all who dwell within Thy universe.

Every being, every creature, every animal, every bird, every manifestation of nature, pays tribute to the constancy and accuracy of Thy unerring laws which have made provision for all that exists in a boundless universe.

All its facets move in concert and rhythm as they obey the dictates of natural law which govern their every motion.

From the stars that swing in their courses, from the earth that revolves on its axis, from the seasons that follow one another, from all growth be it vegetable, fruit, flower or tree, from the actions of all Thy children who bear in miniature some phase of Thy divinity, all pay their tributes to the supreme power, guided by infinite love, which holds the whole universe in its majestic embrace.

We who have seen some of the manifestations of these laws in realms beyond earth, add our pæan of praise, for the passage of time does not dim our wonder, it only increases it and makes us feel with reverence that we should play our part in this cosmic scheme.

And so we strive by precept and example, by dissemination of knowledge, to inculcate into all those who listen and who are ready, those eternal truths which will bring them closer to Thee and to one another and enable them to live their lives in radiance, in dignity, in grandeur and nobility, as they must do when they are conscious of what they are.

Thus shall we help to banish all the darkness that makes for ignorance, bigotry and hatred, all the confusion and chaos, the enmity and greed, the selfish materialism that leads to destruction and usher in that greater kingdom when all will dwell in peace because love reigns and spiritual truths abide.